THE GREAT PROPHETIC BOOKS OF
# Daniel and Revelation

# THE GREAT PROPHETIC BOOKS OF
# Daniel and Revelation

## A BIBLE STUDY JOURNAL

NEW KING JAMES VERSION®

Berrien Springs, Michigan

Andrews University Press
Sutherland House
8360 W. Campus Circle Dr.
Berrien Springs, MI 49104–1700
Telephone: 269–471–6134
Fax: 269–471–6224
Email: aupo@andrews.edu
Website: http://universitypress.andrews.edu

Copyright © 2020 by Andrews University Press

The Holy Bible, New King James Version®
Copyright © 1982 by Thomas Nelson, Inc. Used by permission. All rights reserved.

All rights reserved. No part of this book may be used or reproduced in any manner or translated into other languages without written permission from the publisher except in the case of brief quotations embodied in critical articles and reviews.

Printed in the United States of America

24  23  22  21  20          2  3  4  5

ISBN: 978–1–936337–22–4 (black); 978–1–936337–23–1 (red)

Library of Congress Control Number: 2020931074

# Publisher's Preface

*But you, Daniel, shut up the words, and seal the book until the time of the end; many shall run to and fro, and knowledge shall increase.*
Daniel 12:4

*The Revelation of Jesus Christ, which God gave Him to show His servants—things which must shortly take place. And He sent and signified it by His angel to His servant John, who bore witness to the word of God, and to the testimony of Jesus Christ, to all things that he saw. Blessed is he who reads and those who hear the words of this prophecy, and keep those things which are written in it; for the time is near.*
Revelation 1:1–3

*Every effort is to be made to give the light, not only to our people, but to the world. I have been instructed that the prophecies of Daniel and the Revelation should be printed in small books, with the necessary explanations, and should be sent all over the world.*
Ellen G. White, *Testimonies to the Church*, Vol. 8, 159

*It is several years since light was given me in regard to the need of publishing small books containing Bible stories and others*

> *containing some part of the Bible printed as a whole. . . . The books of Daniel and the Revelation should be bound together and published. A few explanations of certain portions might be added. . . . It was my idea to have the two books bound together, Revelation following Daniel, as giving fuller light on the subjects dealt with in Daniel. The object is to bring these books together, showing that they both relate to the same subjects.*
> Ellen G. White, *The Publishing Ministry*, 313

The four short quotations above, two from Scripture and two from other inspired counsel, succinctly comprise the entire reason why this little volume exists.

The quotation from Daniel, when rightly understood, reminds us that whenever we study the famous prophecies of that book, we are fulfilling that very prophecy. This is a remarkable thought.

Yes, preachers have commonly and understandably used this passage for homiletical purposes to reference the marvels of modern science and technology as a sign of the end. But a literal, exegetical understanding makes it clear that the running to and fro that takes place at the time of the end is a renewed study of the book of Daniel, and that the knowledge that is increased is not that of science or technology, but of a fuller understanding of the prophecies of Daniel themselves. This, of course, is exactly what happened beginning in the late eighteenth century and has increased during the period that these very prophecies have identified as the "time of the end." It is a process that is continuing even as you read these pages. Daniel is a book for our time.

The quotation from Revelation reminds us that God has pronounced a specific blessing on the reading of that book. The reason for that blessing is clearly identified: it is because the events described are near at hand. Who could ever say that it is anything but a blessing to know these great events of heaven and earth even before they take place? Revelation is a book for our time.

The two quotations from Ellen White, obscure and even forgotten though they may have been for the past 120 years, remind us yet again that Daniel and Revelation are to be studied together, because each opens our minds to a fuller understanding of the other and of the great time in history in which we live.

We are pleased to present this as a *Bible study journal*. The *Bible study* part is, of course, the Bible text itself, which we know you will read prayerfully, carefully, and thoughtfully. Along with the Bible text, your study will be enriched by interacting with the corresponding study notes, which have been republished here from the *Andrews Study Bible*. The *journal* part is space specifically reserved for your contribution. You are encouraged to use it freely to record your own notes, insights, discoveries, reflections, and prayers.

It is a special joy in our work as publishers to follow the inspired counsel we have been given. And so this little volume, in this unique format—perhaps unlike anything in the great publishing history of the Advent movement—we are honored to present as *a book for our time*.

Read it. Study it. Fulfill prophecy by doing so. And be blessed by it.

The Publishers
Andrews University Press

# Theological Introduction

Daniel and John wrote their books approximately six hundred years apart, and yet their prophetic insights harmonize perfectly. Both received messages directly communicated by God through an angel in visions or dreams. The content of all prophetic messages in both books covers time from the day of the prophet to the end of time, culminating with the eternal kingdom of God. The same long periods of time are found in both books. They are presented in cycles of discourse that recapitulate and enlarge previous material with new perspectives and insights, allowing for further interpretation and understanding. Both books reveal God's ultimate plan for humanity; thus the prophecies are not conditional. As a result, both are classified as apocalyptic prophecy in which God reveals His foreknowledge and sovereignty, manifesting His unchangeable plan to resolve the problem of sin.

Daniel and Revelation both reveal the great cosmic conflict as the curtain is drawn aside and readers are shown the struggle between God and the powers of evil. Readers are allowed to see how this great controversy, which began in heaven, takes place on earth and how it directly affects the people of God. The issue of worship and thus allegiance lies at the center of this conflict. Satan and his kingdom of evil angels are behind the corrupt social, political, and religious structures on earth, and his forces are ever working to draw attention away from God and toward himself. The message of both books is that God has triumphed and is working His will to make these devilish deceptions plain to all, at which time He will no longer allow them to continue.

Evil will not destroy itself, nor is it destroyed vindictively by God; rather, God's justice and love will intentionally destroy it forever. This is why God instructs His people to be patient. God's people will be victorious only through faithfully worshiping God, who, Himself, is with His people through every moment of time.

The final resolution of the cosmic controversy is intrinsically tied to the sacrifice of Christ, His resurrection, and His ministry in the heavenly sanctuary. His substitutionary role on behalf of all who believe allows His life to take the place of sinners who believe and accept Him as their substitute and submit to His final judgment. This makes the judgment good news to all who believe.

Testing and identifying the profound accuracy of the prophecies as they relate to the geo-political entities through time, readers gain confidence that the unseen portions of the prophecies (mostly those dealing with the pre-advent judgment) are also accurate. God's people are able to locate themselves in the flow of time, which has led those of us living today to understand that we are not far from the end. This provides readers with a sense of hope. The peace and perfect harmony that we will enjoy with the final resolution of the cosmic conflict is near at hand. God's people are called to deliver final warning messages as Noah did before entering the ark. All who believe and do what God has instructed out of love will be liberated from the presence of evil.

Since both Daniel and John saw, in visions, events far distant from their time, God used symbols of familiar objects to convey what could not be comprehended. They begin with a simple image constructed of various metals and clay. They end with a great dragon attacking a woman through two beasts that control the world at the end of time.

The image revealed in Daniel 2 provides the basic historical framework for all other prophecies in both books. Babylon was ruling in the time of Daniel. After Babylon, the combined kingdoms of Media and Persia would arise with Persia being the stronger. Persia would be destroyed by Greece. Rome would conquer Greece and would eventually take on a spiritual and religious character that would exist in an unnatural way until the coming of the everlasting kingdom of God. Four beasts were shown to Daniel (chap. 7) in the second vision, each corresponding to the metals of the image in chapter 2. However, in this vision the religious character of the Roman era was revealed in a little horn that was allowed to persecute God's people for a long period of time. Judgment commenced, which resulted in the destruction of the fourth beast with its little horn and the coming of the kingdom of God. Throughout this vision, Daniel was repeatedly told that the purpose of the vision was to reveal that God's people will be victorious. The vision in chapter 8 contains a new element that reveals the length of time before the judgment but leaves Daniel bewildered. Later, in another vision the angel Gabriel revealed the starting point of that long time period (Dan. 9). Daniel was shown one more vision (Dan. 10), which provided even more details about this long period during which God's people would eventually emerge victorious when Michael, their prince, conquered evil (Dan. 11–12).

John, who lived during the Roman period, was shown (Rev. 1–3) that Jesus Himself is with His people throughout all seven eras of church history from John's day until the coming of the kingdom of God. In this way, the religious character of the Roman period that Daniel saw in the feet of iron and clay and the little horn of chapters 7 and 8, as well as the kings of the north and the south in chapter 11, is expanded upon in greater detail in the book of Revelation. John was then shown the throne room of God (Rev. 4–5). Most of the book of Revelation deals with what he saw in the throne room. He was shown the opening of the seals through all seven church eras (Rev. 6–7) and also the warning trumpet messages given in all seven eras (Rev. 8–11). Daniel's book had been sealed for a time until knowledge concerning the Bible would be increased (Dan. 12:4). During the sixth church era, his book was unsealed (Rev. 10). Then John was shown the cosmic conflict itself (Rev. 12) and its manifestation first in heaven between Michael and Satan and then on earth between God's people (symbolized as a woman, harkening back to Gen. 3:15–16) and Satan (symbolized as a dragon, the serpent from the garden; Gen. 3:14). John saw that Satan was indeed behind all the geopolitical entities from Daniel's time to his own and also behind the rebellious religious element (Rev. 13). John saw that some of God's people were unwittingly in Satan's kingdom (called Babylon) and thus needed to be called out through a series of three final warning messages to the world (Rev. 14). Then, he saw how the great cosmic conflict came to a resolution (Rev. 15–20). Finally, John was allowed to see the peace and harmony of a universe without sin and evil in the final two chapters of the book of Revelation (chaps. 21–22), corresponding to the eternal kingdom of God.

The notes included in this Bible study journal are from the *Andrews Study Bible*. They will provide more detail to help you as you enter into the rewarding study of these two great prophetic books.

# DANIEL

### Daniel and His Friends Obey God
(cf. 2 Kin. 24:10–17)

**1** In the third year of the reign of Jehoiakim king of Judah, Nebuchadnezzar king of Babylon came to Jerusalem and besieged it. ²And the Lord gave Jehoiakim king of Judah into his hand, with some of the articles of ᵃthe house of God, which he carried into the land of Shinar to the house of his god; and he brought the articles into the treasure house of his god.

³Then the king instructed Ashpenaz, the master of his eunuchs, to bring some of the children of Israel and some of the king's descendants and some of the nobles, ⁴young men in whom *there was* no blemish, but good-looking, gifted in all wisdom, possessing knowledge and quick to understand, who *had* ability to serve in the king's palace, and whom they might teach the language and ᵃliterature of the Chaldeans. ⁵And the king appointed for them a daily provision of the king's delicacies and of the wine which he drank, and three years of training for them, so that at the end of *that time* they might serve before the king. ⁶Now from among those of the sons of Judah were Daniel, Hananiah, Mishael, and Azariah. ⁷To them the chief of the eunuchs gave names: he gave Daniel *the name* Belteshazzar; to Hananiah, Shadrach; to Mishael, Meshach; and to Azariah, Abed-Nego.

⁸But Daniel purposed in his heart that he would not defile himself with the portion of the king's delicacies, nor with the

---
1:2 ᵃ The temple    1:4 ᵃ Lit. *writing* or *book*

**1:1—6:28** Interactions among Daniel and his friends and with their God demonstrated to proud monarchs that the Lord rules the world and delivers His people.

**1:1** *third year.* 605 B.C. by Babylonian reckoning, which counted years from April rather than the previous September (Jer. 25:1; 46:2). Thus, from the Babylonian perspective, Jehoiakim's first regnal year began in April 608, not September 609 B.C. **Nebuchadnezzar king of Babylon.** Nebuchadnezzar's father, Nabopolassar, died on August 15, 605 B.C. Daniel was taken captive while Nebuchadnezzar was still the crown prince. His first regnal year began on April 2, 604 B.C. "Babylon" is the Greek form of the word; in Hebrew it appears simply as "Babel," tying this location to that of the postdiluvian tower (Gen. 11:1–9).

**1:2** *some of the articles of the house of God.* The temple remained standing until 586 B.C. But Nebuchadnezzar took some of its valuable items and deposited them in the treasury of his own deity. This introduces conflict between the true God of heaven and human power.

**1:7** *he gave Daniel the name Belteshazzar.* Nebuchadnezzar intended to absorb the young men into his culture by giving them Babylonian identities.

**1:8** *he would not defile himself.* Because Daniel resolved to remain loyal to the Lord, he could not allow himself to be absorbed into Babylonian culture in ways that conflicted with holiness, including eating the meat of "unclean" species of animals (Lev. 11; Deut. 14; compare Gen. 7:2, 8–9). There were probably additional problems with the Babylonian diet: meat may have been slaughtered without properly draining its blood (Gen. 9:4; Lev. 17:10–12; compare Acts 15:20, 29), and food and drink may have been offered to idols (compare Num. 25:2; Acts 15:20, 29).

wine which he drank; therefore he requested of the chief of the eunuchs that he might not defile himself. ⁹Now God had brought Daniel into the favor and ᵃgoodwill of the chief of the eunuchs. ¹⁰And the chief of the eunuchs said to Daniel, "I fear my lord the king, who has appointed your food and drink. For why should he see your faces looking worse than the young men who *are* your age? Then you would endanger my head before the king."

¹¹So Daniel said to ᵃthe steward whom the chief of the eunuchs had set over Daniel, Hananiah, Mishael, and Azariah, ¹²"Please test your servants for ten days, and let them give us vegetables to eat and water to drink. ¹³Then let our appearance be examined before you, and the appearance of the young men who eat the portion of the king's delicacies; and as you see fit, *so* deal with your servants." ¹⁴So he consented with them in this matter, and tested them ten days.

¹⁵And at the end of ten days their features appeared better and fatter in flesh than all the young men who ate the portion of the king's delicacies. ¹⁶Thus ᵃthe steward took away their portion of delicacies and the wine that they were to drink, and gave them vegetables.

¹⁷As for these four young men, God gave them knowledge and skill in all literature and wisdom; and Daniel had understanding in all visions and dreams.

¹⁸Now at the end of the days, when the king had said that they should be brought in, the chief of the eunuchs brought them in before Nebuchadnezzar. ¹⁹Then the king ᵃinterviewed them, and among them all none was found like Daniel, Hananiah, Mishael, and Azariah; therefore they served before the king. ²⁰And in all matters of wisdom *and* understanding about which the king examined them, he found them ten times better than all the magicians *and* astrologers who *were* in all his realm. ²¹Thus Daniel continued until the first year of King Cyrus.

---

1:9 ᵃ *kindness*   1:11 ᵃ Or *Melzar*   1:16 ᵃ Or *Melzar*   1:19 ᵃ Lit. *talked with them*

**1:12 *vegetables . . . water.*** This vegetarian diet would avoid all religious problems (see note on v. 8). It would also be noticeably healthier, which is why Daniel and his friends were allowed to continue it (v. 15). A vegetarian diet is now recognized through research to be nutritionally adequate and useful in both preventing and treating diseases like heart disease, cancer, and type 2 diabetes.

**1:17 *Daniel had understanding in all visions and dreams.*** Daniel was rewarded for his faithfulness to holiness by receiving special access to knowledge from God.

**1:20 *ten times better.*** An expression meaning "very much better." ***than all the magicians and astrologers.*** Daniel and his friends were trained as wise, scholarly counselors to the king alongside various kinds of experts in the use of supernatural forces that were believed to affect human beings.

## Nebuchadnezzar's Dream

**2** Now in the second year of Nebuchadnezzar's reign, Nebuchadnezzar had dreams; and his spirit was *so* troubled that his sleep left him. ²Then the king gave the command to call the magicians, the astrologers, the sorcerers, and the Chaldeans to tell the king his dreams. So they came and stood before the king. ³And the king said to them, "I have had a dream, and my spirit is anxious to ᵃknow the dream."

⁴Then the Chaldeans spoke to the king in Aramaic, "O ᵃ king, live forever! Tell your servants the dream, and we will give the interpretation."

⁵The king answered and said to the Chaldeans, "My ᵃdecision is firm: if you do not make known the dream to me, and its interpretation, you shall be cut in pieces, and your houses shall be made an ash heap. ⁶However, if you tell the dream and its interpretation, you shall receive from me gifts, rewards, and great honor. Therefore tell me the dream and its interpretation."

⁷They answered again and said, "Let the king tell his servants the dream, and we will give its interpretation."

⁸The king answered and said, "I know for certain that you would gain time, because you see that my decision is firm: ⁹if you do not make known the dream to me, *there is only* one decree for you! For you have agreed to speak lying and corrupt words before me till the ᵃtime has changed. Therefore tell me the dream, and I shall know that you can ᵇgive me its interpretation."

¹⁰The Chaldeans answered the king, and said, "There is not a man on earth who can tell the king's matter; therefore no king, lord, or ruler has *ever* asked such things of any magician, astrologer, or Chaldean. ¹¹*It is* a ᵃdifficult thing that the king requests, and there is no other who can tell it to the king except the gods, whose dwelling is not with flesh."

---

**2:3** ᵃ Or *understand*   **2:4** ᵃ The original language of Daniel 2:4b through 7:28 is Aramaic.   **2:5** ᵃ The command   **2:9** ᵃ Situation   ᵇ Or *declare to me*   **2:11** ᵃ Or *rare*

**2:1 *second year of Nebuchadnezzar's reign.*** This could have been just after Daniel and his friends completed their three years of training (1:5, 18). Their training would have started before the first official year of Nebuchadnezzar's reign began in the spring of 604 B.C.

**2:4 *O king.*** Here the original language changes from Hebrew to Aramaic.

¹²For this reason the king was angry and very furious, and gave the command to destroy all the wise *men* of Babylon. ¹³So the decree went out, and they began killing the wise *men;* and they sought Daniel and his companions, to kill *them.*

**God Reveals Nebuchadnezzar's Dream**

¹⁴Then with counsel and wisdom Daniel answered Arioch, the captain of the king's guard, who had gone out to kill the wise *men* of Babylon; ¹⁵he answered and said to Arioch the king's captain, "Why is the decree from the king so ᵃurgent?" Then Arioch made the decision known to Daniel.

¹⁶So Daniel went in and asked the king to give him time, that he might tell the king the interpretation. ¹⁷Then Daniel went to his house, and made the decision known to Hananiah, Mishael, and Azariah, his companions, ¹⁸that they might seek mercies from the God of heaven concerning this secret, so that Daniel and his companions might not perish with the rest of the wise *men* of Babylon. ¹⁹Then the secret was revealed to Daniel in a night vision. So Daniel blessed the God of heaven.

²⁰Daniel answered and said:

"Blessed be the name of God forever and ever,
 For wisdom and might are His.
21 And He changes the times and the seasons;
 He removes kings and raises up kings;
 He gives wisdom to the wise
 And knowledge to those who have understanding.
22 He reveals deep and secret things;
 He knows what *is* in the darkness,
 And light dwells with Him.

23 "I thank You and praise You,
 O God of my fathers;
 You have given me wisdom and might,

---

2:15 ᵃ Or *harsh*

And have now made known to me what we asked of You,
For You have made known to us the king's ᵃdemand."

## Daniel Explains the Dream

²⁴Therefore Daniel went to Arioch, whom the king had appointed to destroy the wise *men* of Babylon. He went and said thus to him: "Do not destroy the wise *men* of Babylon; take me before the king, and I will tell the king the interpretation."

²⁵Then Arioch quickly brought Daniel before the king, and said thus to him, "I have found a man of the ᵃcaptives of Judah, who will make known to the king the interpretation."

²⁶The king answered and said to Daniel, whose name *was* Belteshazzar, "Are you able to make known to me the dream which I have seen, and its interpretation?"

²⁷Daniel answered in the presence of the king, and said, "The secret which the king has demanded, the wise *men,* the astrologers, the magicians, and the soothsayers cannot declare to the king. ²⁸But there is a God in heaven who reveals secrets, and He has made known to King Nebuchadnezzar what will be in the latter days. Your dream, and the visions of your head upon your bed, were these: ²⁹As for you, O king, thoughts came *to* your *mind while* on your bed, *about* what would come to pass after this; and He who reveals secrets has made known to you what will be. ³⁰But as for me, this secret has not been revealed to me because I have more wisdom than anyone living, but for *our* sakes who make known the interpretation to the king, and that you may ᵃknow the thoughts of your heart.

³¹"You, O king, were watching; and behold, a great image! This great image, whose splendor *was* excellent, stood before you; and its form *was* awesome. ³²This image's head *was* of fine gold, its chest and arms of silver, its belly and ᵃthighs of bronze, ³³its legs of iron, its feet partly of iron and partly of ᵃclay.

---

2:23 ᵃ Lit. *word*   2:25 ᵃ Lit. *sons of the captivity*   2:30 ᵃ Understand   2:32 ᵃ Or *sides*   2:33 ᵃ Or *baked clay,* also vv. 34, 35, 42

**2:28 what will be in the latter days.** Compare Num. 24:14; Ezek. 38:16. Nebuchadnezzar's dream moved forward to the time when God Himself would set up His kingdom on earth (Dan. 2:37–44).

**2:31 a great image.** Appropriate for representing a succession of temporary human governments.

³⁴You watched while a stone was cut out without hands, which struck the image on its feet of iron and clay, and broke them in pieces. ³⁵Then the iron, the clay, the bronze, the silver, and the gold were crushed together, and became like chaff from the summer threshing floors; the wind carried them away so that no trace of them was found. And the stone that struck the image became a great mountain and filled the whole earth.

³⁶"This *is* the dream. Now we will tell the interpretation of it before the king. ³⁷You, O king, *are* a king of kings. For the God of heaven has given you a kingdom, power, strength, and glory; ³⁸and wherever the children of men dwell, or the beasts of the field and the birds of the heaven, He has given *them* into your hand, and has made you ruler over them all—you *are* this head of gold. ³⁹But after you shall arise another kingdom inferior to yours; then another, a third kingdom of bronze, which shall rule

**2:38 you are this head of gold.** The fact that Daniel identified the first segment of the image as Nebuchadnezzar's Neo-Babylonian kingdom (605–539 B.C.), of which he was the current monarch, provides a historical anchor point for identifying the following kingdoms (compare 8:20–21).

**2:39 after you shall arise another kingdom.** The fact that a kingdom came after Nebuchadnezzar's head of gold indicates that the head also represented a kingdom, which included Nebuchadnezzar (605–562 B.C.) and several lesser Neo-Babylonian rulers who followed him (562–539 B.C.). **inferior to yours.** This inferiority, represented by the decreasing value of metals, could not refer to geographical extent, military might (note the increasing hardness of metals; compare v. 40; 7:7), or overall wealth, which increased from one empire to another. However, it could refer to the glory of its capital city (Babylon is legendary), culture, and especially moral worth, as human rulers became progressively more corrupt, arrogant, and rebellious against God. **a third kingdom of bronze.** Alexander the Great (336–323 B.C.) conquered Medo-Persia and set up a Macedonian/Greek Empire (330–30 B.C.; see 8:20–22). **which shall rule over all the earth.** Alexander's empire was notable for its vast extent. But "all the earth" does not literally refer to the totality of planet Earth. Nor does it mean "the then-known world." This and all other empires had limits, and those inside knew about peoples outside, with whom they warred or traded. There were great empires elsewhere, such as a Chinese Empire that rivaled the Roman Empire in extent and power. But the empires in Dan. 2 were those that controlled the promised land and affected God's people.

| Empires in the Book of Daniel | | | |
|---|---|---|---|
| **Nebuchadnezzar's Dream: The Great Image (chap. 2)** | **Daniel's Dream: The Four Great Beasts (chap. 7)** | **Daniel's Vision: The Ram and the Goat (chap. 8)** | **Explanation: Four World Empires** |
| Head of fine gold | Lion with eagle's wings | | Babylon (2:38; 7:17) |
| Chest and arms of silver | Bear raised up on one side, with three ribs in its mouth | Ram with two horns, one longer than the other | Medo-Persia (2:39; 7:17; 8:20) |
| Belly and thighs of bronze | Leopard with four wings of a bird and four heads | Male goat with a notable horn between his eyes. The large horn was broken and replaced with four horns | Greece (2:39; 7:17; 8:21). Later divided into four kingdoms (8:22) |
| Legs of iron and feet partly of iron and partly of clay | Unidentified beast with iron teeth, ten horns, and a little horn, having eyes of a man and a mouth | Little horn growing exceedingly great | Rome (2:40) |

over all the earth. **⁴⁰**And the fourth kingdom shall be as strong as iron, inasmuch as iron breaks in pieces and shatters everything; and like iron that crushes, *that kingdom* will break in pieces and crush all the others. **⁴¹**Whereas you saw the feet and toes, partly of potter's clay and partly of iron, the kingdom shall be divided; yet the strength of the iron shall be in it, just as you saw the iron mixed with ceramic clay. **⁴²**And *as* the toes of the feet *were* partly of iron and partly of clay, *so* the kingdom shall be partly strong and partly ᵃfragile. **⁴³**As you saw iron mixed with ceramic clay, they will mingle with the seed of men; but they will not adhere to one another, just as iron does not mix with clay. **⁴⁴**And in the days of these kings the God of heaven will set up a kingdom which shall never be destroyed; and the kingdom shall not be left to other people; it shall ᵃbreak in pieces and ᵇconsume all these kingdoms, and it shall stand forever. **⁴⁵**Inasmuch as you saw that the stone was cut out of the mountain without hands, and that it broke in pieces the iron, the bronze, the clay, the silver, and the gold—the great God has made known to the king what will come to pass after this. The dream is certain, and its interpretation is sure."

### Daniel and His Friends Promoted

**⁴⁶**Then King Nebuchadnezzar fell on his face, prostrate before Daniel, and commanded that they should present an offering and incense to him. **⁴⁷**The king answered Daniel, and said, "Truly your God *is* the God of gods, the Lord of kings, and a revealer of secrets, since you could reveal this secret." **⁴⁸**Then the king promoted Daniel and gave him many great gifts; and he made him ruler over the whole province of Babylon, and chief administrator over all the wise *men* of Babylon. **⁴⁹**Also Daniel petitioned the king, and he set Shadrach, Meshach, and Abed-Nego over the affairs of the province of Babylon; but Daniel *sat* in ᵃthe gate of the king.

---

**2:42** ᵃ Or *brittle*   **2:44** ᵃ Or *crush*   ᵇ Lit. *put an end to*   **2:49** ᵃ The king's court

**2:40 the fourth kingdom shall be as strong as iron.** Between 168 and 30 B.C., Rome took over the Greek kingdoms into which Alexander's empire was divided (compare 8:8, 22). Rome was the strongest and lasted the longest of the four kingdoms represented in Daniel's image.

**2:41 the kingdom shall be divided.** The Roman emperor Constantine divided the empire into western and eastern parts (A.D. 326). Then the western part fell to barbarians and was divided into a number of European countries, which have varied in strength. The eastern part of the Roman Empire continued as the Byzantine Empire, which was conquered by Muslims in A.D. 1453.

**2:43 they will not adhere to one another.** The remnants of the Roman Empire have never been successfully reunited, despite major efforts for centuries through warfare and political marriages.

**2:44 in the days of these kings the God of heaven.** Sometime during the current period of divided powers, God will suddenly intervene (as represented by the stone smashing the image; vv. 34–35, 45) and set up His eternal kingdom throughout the whole world. The NT identifies Christ's Second Coming as the cause of this sudden and universally recognized end of human civilization as we know it (Matt. 24:23–51; Rev. 19:11–21).

**2:46 present an offering and incense to him.** Apparently Nebuchadnezzar tried to treat Daniel as divine (compare Acts 14:11–18), although he praised Daniel's God (Dan. 2:47). Undoubtedly Daniel would have directed the king's worship to God (compare vv. 28–30, 45).

## The Image of Gold

**3** Nebuchadnezzar the king made an image of gold, whose height *was* <sup>a</sup>sixty cubits *and* its width six cubits. He set it up in the plain of Dura, in the province of Babylon. ²And King Nebuchadnezzar sent *word* to gather together the satraps, the administrators, the governors, the counselors, the treasurers, the judges, the magistrates, and all the officials of the provinces, to come to the dedication of the image which King Nebuchadnezzar had set up. ³So the satraps, the administrators, the governors, the counselors, the treasurers, the judges, the magistrates, and all the officials of the provinces gathered together for the dedication of the image that King Nebuchadnezzar had set up; and they stood before the image that Nebuchadnezzar had set up. ⁴Then a herald cried <sup>a</sup>aloud: "To you it is commanded, O peoples, nations, and languages, ⁵*that* at the time you hear the sound of the horn, flute, harp, lyre, *and* psaltery, in symphony with all kinds of music, you shall fall down and worship the gold image that King Nebuchadnezzar has set up; ⁶and whoever does not fall down and worship shall be cast immediately into the midst of a burning fiery furnace."

⁷So at that time, when all the people heard the sound of the horn, flute, harp, *and* lyre, in symphony with all kinds of music, all the people, nations, and languages fell down *and* worshiped the gold image which King Nebuchadnezzar had set up.

## Daniel's Friends Disobey the King

⁸Therefore at that time certain Chaldeans came forward and accused the Jews. ⁹They spoke and said to King Nebuchadnezzar, "O king, live forever! ¹⁰You, O king, have made a decree that everyone who hears the sound of the horn, flute, harp, lyre, *and* psaltery, in symphony with all kinds of music, shall fall down and worship the gold image; ¹¹and whoever does not fall down and worship shall be cast into the midst of a burning fiery furnace. ¹²There are certain Jews whom you have set over the affairs of

---

**3:1** <sup>a</sup> About 90 feet   **3:4** <sup>a</sup> Lit. *with strength*

**3:1 height . . . sixty cubits and its width six cubits.** About 90 feet (27 m) high and 9 feet (2.7 m) wide.

**3:2 dedication of the image.** Consecration of the statue as a sacred object (vv. 12, 14, 28; compare dedication of the Lord's temple in Ezra 6:16–18). Apparently it represented Nebuchadnezzar, the "head of gold" (Dan. 2:38), and/or his gods (3:12). In rebelling against God's power, he twisted his dream (chap. 2) to serve his own ambition.

**3:3 So the satraps . . . all the officials.** The list gives an atmosphere of pomp and prolongs the story to heighten suspense.

**3:5 all kinds of music.** Compare the use of instruments for Israelite worship (2 Sam. 6:5, 15; 1 Chr. 25) or for religious signals (Num. 10:10). Nebuchadnezzar had an entire ancient symphony orchestra. The names of three of the instruments in Dan. 3 are Greek and the others are Persian. This is not surprising because Babylonia was in contact with other cultures.

**3:6 burning fiery furnace.** Perhaps it was like a kiln for baking bricks. The fact that Nebuchadnezzar threatened such punishment could imply that he doubted whether everyone was sufficiently loyal to him.

the province of Babylon: Shadrach, Meshach, and Abed-Nego; these men, O king, have not paid due regard to you. They do not serve your gods or worship the gold image which you have set up."

<sup>13</sup>Then Nebuchadnezzar, in rage and fury, gave the command to bring Shadrach, Meshach, and Abed-Nego. So they brought these men before the king. <sup>14</sup>Nebuchadnezzar spoke, saying to them, "*Is it* true, Shadrach, Meshach, and Abed-Nego, *that* you do not serve my gods or worship the gold image which I have set up? <sup>15</sup>Now if you are ready at the time you hear the sound of the horn, flute, harp, lyre, *and* psaltery, in symphony with all kinds of music, and you fall down and worship the image which I have made, *good!* But if you do not worship, you shall be cast immediately into the midst of a burning fiery furnace. And who *is* the god who will deliver you from my hands?"

<sup>16</sup>Shadrach, Meshach, and Abed-Nego answered and said to the king, "O Nebuchadnezzar, we have no need to answer you in this matter. <sup>17</sup>If that *is the case,* our God whom we serve is able to deliver us from the burning fiery furnace, and He will deliver *us* from your hand, O king. <sup>18</sup>But if not, let it be known to you, O king, that we do not serve your gods, nor will we worship the gold image which you have set up."

### Saved in Fiery Trial

<sup>19</sup>Then Nebuchadnezzar was full of fury, and the expression on his face changed toward Shadrach, Meshach, and Abed-Nego. He spoke and commanded that they heat the furnace seven times more than it was usually heated. <sup>20</sup>And he commanded certain mighty men of valor who *were* in his army to bind Shadrach, Meshach, and Abed-Nego, *and* cast *them* into the burning fiery furnace. <sup>21</sup>Then these men were bound in their coats, their trousers, their turbans, and their *other* garments, and were cast into the midst of the burning fiery furnace. <sup>22</sup>Therefore, because the king's command was <sup>a</sup>urgent, and the furnace exceedingly hot,

---

**3:22** <sup>a</sup> Or *harsh*

**3:13 *in rage and fury.*** Understandable because Nebuchadnezzar was trying to stage a 100 percent show of absolute personal loyalty to himself from his subjects.

**3:15 *who is the god who will deliver you.*** Intended as a rhetorical question with the answer: no god. But the young Jews had a different answer (v. 17).

**3:18 *But if not.*** They would trust God, even if He allowed them to be killed (compare Job 13:15; Matt. 26:39; Acts 7:59).

the flame of the fire killed those men who took up Shadrach, Meshach, and Abed-Nego. ²³And these three men, Shadrach, Meshach, and Abed-Nego, fell down bound into the midst of the burning fiery furnace.

²⁴Then King Nebuchadnezzar was astonished; and he rose in haste *and* spoke, saying to his [a]counselors, "Did we not cast three men bound into the midst of the fire?"

They answered and said to the king, "True, O king."

²⁵"Look!" he answered, "I see four men loose, walking in the midst of the fire; and they are not hurt, and the form of the fourth is like the [a] Son of God."

## Nebuchadnezzar Praises God

²⁶Then Nebuchadnezzar went near the [a]mouth of the burning fiery furnace *and* spoke, saying, "Shadrach, Meshach, and Abed-Nego, servants of the Most High God, come out, and come *here*." Then Shadrach, Meshach, and Abed-Nego came from the midst of the fire. ²⁷And the satraps, administrators, governors, and the king's counselors gathered together, and they saw these men on whose bodies the fire had no power; the hair of their head was not singed nor were their garments affected, and the smell of fire was not on them.

²⁸Nebuchadnezzar spoke, saying, "Blessed be the God of Shadrach, Meshach, and Abed-Nego, who sent His Angel[a] and delivered His servants who trusted in Him, and they have frustrated the king's word, and yielded their bodies, that they should not serve nor worship any god except their own God! ²⁹Therefore I make a decree that any people, nation, or language which speaks anything amiss against the God of Shadrach, Meshach, and Abed-Nego shall be cut in pieces, and their houses shall be made an ash heap; because there is no other God who can deliver like this."

3:24 [a] High officials   3:25 [a] Or *a son of the gods*   3:26 [a] Lit. *door*   3:28 [a] Or *angel*

**3:25 the Son of God.** Or "a son of the gods," that is, a divine being. This was from Nebuchadnezzar's religious perspective. The being was Christ, the pre-incarnate. He literally fulfilled God's promise to be with His people in order to deliver them: "When you walk through the fire, you shall not be burned, nor shall the flame scorch you" (Is. 43:2).

**3:28 Blessed be the God.** The king realized that the young men's disobedience was due to their amazing loyalty to their unique deity, not a rebellion against his human rule of Babylon. So he protected the honor of their God and promoted them (vv. 29–30). **who sent His Angel.** The word "angel" means "messenger" and can be divine (Judg. 6:11–13—"Angel of the Lord"). It is not restricted to created beings.

30 Then the king ᵃpromoted Shadrach, Meshach, and Abed-Nego in the province of Babylon.

**Nebuchadnezzar's Second Dream**

  Nebuchadnezzar the king,

To all peoples, nations, and languages that dwell in all the earth:

Peace be multiplied to you.

2   I thought it good to declare the signs and wonders that the Most High God has worked for me.

3   How great *are* His signs,
And how mighty His wonders!
His kingdom *is* an everlasting kingdom,
And His dominion *is* from generation to generation.

4   I, Nebuchadnezzar, was at rest in my house, and flourishing in my palace. ⁵I saw a dream which made me afraid, and the thoughts on my bed and the visions of my head troubled me. ⁶Therefore I issued a decree to bring in all the wise *men* of Babylon before me, that they might make known to me the interpretation of the dream. ⁷Then the magicians, the astrologers, the Chaldeans, and the soothsayers came in, and I told them the dream; but they did not make known to me its interpretation. ⁸But at last Daniel came before me (his name *is* Belteshazzar, according to the name of my god; in him *is* the Spirit of the Holy God), and I told the dream before him, *saying:* ⁹"Belteshazzar, chief of the magicians, because I know that the Spirit of the Holy God *is* in you, and no secret troubles you, explain to me the visions of my dream that I have seen, and its interpretation.

---

3:30 ᵃ Lit. *caused to prosper*

**4:1 To all peoples, nations, and languages.** This chapter begins as a letter by Nebuchadnezzar to the inhabitants of his kingdom. He expresses interest in the well-being of his subjects and acknowledges the supremacy of the Lord's power (compare chap. 2).

**4:4 I, Nebuchadnezzar.** The king recounts the experience that led to his praise for Daniel's God.

**4:8 in him is the Spirit of the Holy God.** Compare Gen. 41:38.

¹⁰ "These *were* the visions of my head *while* on my bed:

I was looking, and behold,
A tree in the midst of the earth,
And its height was great.
¹¹ The tree grew and became strong;
Its height reached to the heavens,
And it could be seen to the ends of all the earth.
¹² Its leaves *were* lovely,
Its fruit abundant,
And in it *was* food for all.
The beasts of the field found shade under it,
The birds of the heavens dwelt in its branches,
And all flesh was fed from it.

¹³ "I saw in the visions of my head *while* on my bed, and there was a watcher, a holy one, coming down from heaven. ¹⁴He cried [a] aloud and said thus:

'Chop down the tree and cut off its branches,
Strip off its leaves and scatter its fruit.
Let the beasts get out from under it,
And the birds from its branches.
¹⁵ Nevertheless leave the stump and roots in the earth,
*Bound* with a band of iron and bronze,
In the tender grass of the field.
Let it be wet with the dew of heaven,
And *let* him graze with the beasts
On the grass of the earth.
¹⁶ Let his heart be changed from *that of* a man,
Let him be given the heart of a beast,
And let seven times [a] pass over him.

¹⁷ 'This decision *is* by the decree of the watchers,

---

**4:14** [a] Lit. *with strength*    **4:16** [a] Possibly *years*

**4:13 *a watcher, a holy one.*** A supernatural being (angel) serving God.

And the sentence by the word of the holy ones,
In order that the living may know
That the Most High rules in the kingdom of men,
Gives it to whomever He will,
And sets over it the lowest of men.'

<sup>18</sup> "This dream I, King Nebuchadnezzar, have seen. Now you, Belteshazzar, declare its interpretation, since all the wise *men* of my kingdom are not able to make known to me the interpretation; but you *are* able, for the Spirit of the Holy God *is* in you."

### Daniel Explains the Second Dream

<sup>19</sup> Then Daniel, whose name *was* Belteshazzar, was astonished for a time, and his thoughts troubled him. *So* the king spoke, and said, "Belteshazzar, do not let the dream or its interpretation trouble you."
Belteshazzar answered and said, "My lord, *may* the dream <sup>a</sup>concern those who hate you, and its interpretation <sup>b</sup>concern your enemies!

<sup>20</sup> "The tree that you saw, which grew and became strong, whose height reached to the heavens and which *could be* seen by all the earth, <sup>21</sup>whose leaves *were* lovely and its fruit abundant, in which *was* food for all, under which the beasts of the field dwelt, and in whose branches the birds of the heaven had their home— <sup>22</sup>it *is* you, O king, who have grown and become strong; for your greatness has grown and reaches to the heavens, and your dominion to the end of the earth.

<sup>23</sup> "And inasmuch as the king saw a watcher, a holy one, coming down from heaven and saying, 'Chop down the tree and destroy it, but leave its stump and roots in the earth, *bound* with a band of iron and bronze in the tender grass of the field;

---

4:19 <sup>a</sup> be for   <sup>b</sup> for

let it be wet with the dew of heaven, and let him graze with the beasts of the field, till seven ᵃtimes pass over him'; ²⁴this is the interpretation, O king, and this is the decree of the Most High, which has come upon my lord the king: ²⁵They shall drive you from men, your dwelling shall be with the beasts of the field, and they shall make you eat grass like oxen. They shall wet you with the dew of heaven, and seven ᵃtimes shall pass over you, till you know that the Most High rules in the kingdom of men, and gives it to whomever He chooses.

²⁶ "And inasmuch as they gave the command to leave the stump *and* roots of the tree, your kingdom shall be assured to you, after you come to know that Heavenᵃ rules. ²⁷Therefore, O king, let my advice be acceptable to you; break off your sins by *being* righteous, and your iniquities by showing mercy to *the* poor. Perhaps there may be a ᵃlengthening of your prosperity."

**Nebuchadnezzar's Humiliation**

²⁸ All *this* came upon King Nebuchadnezzar. ²⁹At the end of the twelve months he was walking ᵃabout the royal palace of Babylon. ³⁰The king spoke, saying, "Is not this great Babylon, that I have built for a royal dwelling by my mighty power and for the honor of my majesty?"

³¹ While the word *was still* in the king's mouth, a voice fell from heaven: "King Nebuchadnezzar, to you it is spoken: the kingdom has departed from you! ³²And they shall drive you from men, and your dwelling *shall be* with the beasts of the field. They shall make you eat grass like oxen; and seven ᵃtimes shall pass over you, until you know that the Most High rules in the kingdom of men, and gives it to whomever He chooses."

---

4:23 ᵃ Possibly *years*   4:25 ᵃ Possibly *years*   4:26 ᵃ God   4:27 ᵃ *prolonging*   4:29 ᵃ Or *upon*
4:32 ᵃ Possibly *years*

**4:27 let my advice.** Daniel hoped the divine sentence could be put off if the king would walk humbly with God by doing justice and loving mercy (compare Mic. 6:8).

**4:30 great Babylon, that I have built.** Accurate from a human perspective. Nebuchadnezzar was an incredible builder and made Babylon—with its hanging gardens, walls, palaces, and temples—into a wonder of the ancient world. But pride led him to arrogantly overlook his debt and accountability to God.

**4:32–33 seven times . . . his nails like birds' claws.** Such growth implies a considerable length of time, implying that the "seven times" of Nebuchadnezzar's madness were seven years. The Aramaic word for "time" also means year.

³³ That very hour the word was fulfilled concerning Nebuchadnezzar; he was driven from men and ate grass like oxen; his body was wet with the dew of heaven till his hair had grown like eagles' *feathers* and his nails like birds' *claws*.

### Nebuchadnezzar Praises God

³⁴ And at the end of the ᵃtime I, Nebuchadnezzar, lifted my eyes to heaven, and my understanding returned to me; and I blessed the Most High and praised and honored Him who lives forever:

For His dominion *is* an everlasting dominion,
And His kingdom *is* from generation to generation.
³⁵ All the inhabitants of the earth *are* reputed as nothing;
He does according to His will in the army of heaven
And *among* the inhabitants of the earth.
No one can restrain His hand
Or say to Him, "What have You done?"

³⁶ At the same time my reason returned to me, and for the glory of my kingdom, my honor and splendor returned to me. My counselors and nobles resorted to me, I was restored to my kingdom, and excellent majesty was added to me. ³⁷Now I, Nebuchadnezzar, praise and extol and honor the King of heaven, all of whose works *are* truth, and His ways justice. And those who walk in pride He is able to put down.

### Belshazzar's Feast

**5** Belshazzar the king made a great feast for a thousand of his lords, and drank wine in the presence of the thousand. ²While he tasted the wine, Belshazzar gave the command to bring the gold and silver vessels which his ᵃfather Nebuchadnezzar had taken from the temple which *had been* in Jerusalem, that the king and his lords, his wives, and his concubines might drink

---

4:34 ᵃ Lit. *days*   5:2 ᵃ Or *ancestor*

**4:37 praise and extol and honor the King of heaven.** The message of God's sovereignty finally sank in when Nebuchadnezzar was first removed from his throne and then restored (compare 2 Chr. 33:11–13).

**5:1 Belshazzar the king.** Belshazzar co-reigned with his father, Nabonidus (555–539 B.C.), during the last ten years of his reign. Because only Nabonidus was mentioned in later Greek historical writings as the last king of Babylon, scholars regarded the book of Daniel as inaccurate and unreliable. However, discovery of Babylonian texts has confirmed the existence and kingship of Belshazzar. So Daniel records accurate information that was lost for many centuries. This helps scholars establish an understanding of when the book of Daniel was written. **great feast.** Belshazzar and his subjects thought they were secure within the immense fortifications of their city. By hosting a feast, Belshazzar apparently tried to maintain his people's morale at a time of crisis while the Medo-Persian army was approaching.

**5:2 command to bring the gold and silver vessels.** Under the influence of alcohol that clouded his judgment (compare Lev. 10:9–10; Matt. 14:6–11), Belshazzar commanded improper use of the Lord's temple vessels, apparently to boost confidence by showing that the Babylonian gods were superior. **his father.** Can also mean "ancestor." His mother was probably the daughter of Nebuchadnezzar (see note on v. 1 and v. 11).

from them. ³Then they brought the gold vessels that had been taken from the temple of the house of God which *had been* in Jerusalem; and the king and his lords, his wives, and his concubines drank from them. ⁴They drank wine, and praised the gods of gold and silver, bronze and iron, wood and stone.

⁵In the same hour the fingers of a man's hand appeared and wrote opposite the lampstand on the plaster of the wall of the king's palace; and the king saw the part of the hand that wrote. ⁶Then the king's countenance changed, and his thoughts troubled him, so that the joints of his hips were loosened and his knees knocked against each other. ⁷The king cried ᵃaloud to bring in the astrologers, the Chaldeans, and the soothsayers. The king spoke, saying to the wise *men* of Babylon, "Whoever reads this writing, and tells me its interpretation, shall be clothed with purple and *have* a chain of gold around his neck; and he shall be the third ruler in the kingdom." ⁸Now all the king's wise *men* came, but they could not read the writing, or make known to the king its interpretation. ⁹Then King Belshazzar was greatly troubled, his countenance was changed, and his lords were ᵃastonished.

¹⁰The queen, because of the words of the king and his lords, came to the banquet hall. The queen spoke, saying, "O king, live forever! Do not let your thoughts trouble you, nor let your countenance change. ¹¹There is a man in your kingdom in whom *is* the Spirit of the Holy God. And in the days of your ᵃfather, light and understanding and wisdom, like the wisdom of the gods, were found in him; and King Nebuchadnezzar your ᵃfather—your father the king—made him chief of the magicians, astrologers, Chaldeans, *and* soothsayers. ¹²Inasmuch as an excellent spirit, knowledge, understanding, interpreting dreams, solving riddles, and ᵃexplaining enigmas were found in this Daniel, whom the king named Belteshazzar, now let Daniel be called, and he will give the interpretation."

---

5:7 ᵃ Lit. *with strength*   5:9 ᵃ *perplexed*   5:11 ᵃ Or ancestor   5:12 ᵃ Lit. *untying knots*

**5:4 *gold . . . iron.*** The sequence of metals reminds readers that a change is coming (2:37–40).

**5:5 *fingers of a man's hand appeared and wrote.*** The Babylonians would likely have viewed this as a deity recording their fate.

**5:10 *The queen.*** This could be the queen-mother, Belshazzar's grandmother, who may have belonged to Nebuchadnezzar's harem.

**5:11 *King Nebuchadnezzar your father.*** Compare v. 22. Here "father" may mean "grandfather," "step-grandfather," or simply "previous king of Babylon." Nabu-(zer)-usabsi, Nabonidus's father, was the brother of Nebuchadnezzar, which made him Belshazzar's granduncle through Nabonidus (see Jer. 27:6–7). But it is likely that Nebuchadnezzar was his grandfather through Belshazzar's mother (see note on v. 2).

## The Writing on the Wall Explained

**13**Then Daniel was brought in before the king. The king spoke, and said to Daniel, "*Are* you that Daniel ᵃwho is one of the captives from Judah, whom my ᵇfather the king brought from Judah? **14**I have heard of you, that the ᵃSpirit of God *is* in you, and *that* light and understanding and excellent wisdom are found in you. **15**Now the wise *men,* the astrologers, have been brought in before me, that they should read this writing and make known to me its interpretation, but they could not give the interpretation of the thing. **16**And I have heard of you, that you can give interpretations and ᵃexplain enigmas. Now if you can read the writing and make known to me its interpretation, you shall be clothed with purple and *have* a chain of gold around your neck, and shall be the third ruler in the kingdom."

**17**Then Daniel answered, and said before the king, "Let your gifts be for yourself, and give your rewards to another; yet I will read the writing to the king, and make known to him the interpretation. **18**O king, the Most High God gave Nebuchadnezzar your ᵃfather a kingdom and majesty, glory and honor. **19**And because of the majesty that He gave him, all peoples, nations, and languages trembled and feared before him. Whomever he wished, he executed; whomever he wished, he kept alive; whomever he wished, he set up; and whomever he wished, he put down. **20**But when his heart was lifted up, and his spirit was hardened in pride, he was deposed from his kingly throne, and they took his glory from him. **21**Then he was driven from the sons of men, his heart was made like the beasts, and his dwelling *was* with the wild donkeys. They fed him with grass like oxen, and his body was wet with the dew of heaven, till he ᵃknew that the Most High God rules in the kingdom of men, and appoints over it whomever He chooses.

**22**"But you his son, Belshazzar, have not humbled your heart, although you knew all this. **23**And you have ᵃlifted yourself up against the Lord of heaven. They have brought the vessels of ᵇHis

---

5:13 ᵃ Lit. *who is of the sons of the captivity*  ᵇ Or *ancestor*  5:14 ᵃ Or *spirit of the gods*  5:16 ᵃ Lit. *untie knots*  5:18 ᵃ Or *ancestor*  5:21 ᵃ Recognized  5:23 ᵃ Exalted  ᵇ The temple

house before you, and you and your lords, your wives and your concubines, have drunk wine from them. And you have praised the gods of silver and gold, bronze and iron, wood and stone, which do not see or hear or know; and the God who *holds* your breath in His hand and owns all your ways, you have not glorified. ²⁴Then the ᵃfingers of the hand were sent from Him, and this writing was written.

²⁵"And this is the inscription that was written:

> ᵃMENE, MENE, ᵇTEKEL, ᶜUPHARSIN.

²⁶This *is* the interpretation of *each* word. Mene: God has numbered your kingdom, and finished it; ²⁷Tekel: You have been weighed in the balances, and found wanting; ²⁸Peres: Your kingdom has been divided, and given to the Medes and Persians." ᵃ ²⁹Then Belshazzar gave the command, and they clothed Daniel with purple and *put* a chain of gold around his neck, and made a proclamation concerning him that he should be the third ruler in the kingdom.

### Belshazzar's Fall

³⁰That very night Belshazzar, king of the Chaldeans, was slain. ³¹And Darius the Mede received the kingdom, *being* about sixty-two years old.

### The Plot Against Daniel

**6** It pleased Darius to set over the kingdom one hundred and twenty satraps, to be over the whole kingdom; ²and over these, three governors, of whom Daniel *was* one, that the satraps might give account to them, so that the king would suffer no loss. ³Then this Daniel distinguished himself above the governors and satraps, because an excellent spirit *was* in him; and the king gave thought to setting him over the whole realm. ⁴So the governors

---

5:24 ᵃ Lit. *palm*   5:25 ᵃ Lit. *a mina* (50 shekels) from the verb "to number"   ᵇ Lit. *a shekel* from the verb "to weigh"   ᶜ Lit. *and half-shekels* from the verb "to divide"; pl. of *Peres*, v. 28   5:28 ᵃ Aram. *Paras*, consonant with *Peres*

**5:23 the God who holds your breath in His hand.** God's creative power continually sustains His creatures (compare Job 12:10; Ps. 104:14–15; 145:15–16).

**5:25 MENE, MENE, TEKEL, UPHARSIN.** These words are in Aramaic but share some roots with the Babylonian language. They refer to units of weight that were used for money: "mina, mina, shekel [1/60 of a mina], and half-minas [or half-shekels]." The handwriting on the wall was a riddle that would sound to us something like "dollar, dollar, penny, and half-dollars." Weights were appropriate in this context because they were weighed in balances (v. 27). Money was appropriate because all the wealth of Babylon could not ransom it from destruction because it was morally bankrupt. Beyond the initial impact of the riddle, the underlying roots of the words for weights refer to how he and his kingdom were "numbered," "weighed," and "divided." Daniel explained how God applied these actions to the ruler and kingdom that were under divine judgment (vv. 26–28).

**5:29 third ruler.** Why not the second ruler, which is what Pharaoh made Joseph (Gen. 41:40)? Perhaps because Belshazzar himself was second ruler to his father Nabonidus, with whom he was co-reigning. So this verse may imply the existence of Nabonidus, although the book of Daniel does not directly mention him.

**5:31 Darius the Mede received the kingdom.** Cyrus II the Great (reigned 559–530 B.C.; see also 1:21; 6:28; 10:1), the Persian who founded the Achaemenid Medo-Persian Empire, conquered Babylon in 539 B.C. (compare Rev. 16:12). "Darius the Mede" is not mentioned, at least not by this name, in ancient writings outside the Bible that have been discovered so far. This could be a throne name for Gaubaruwa (Babylonian Gubaru/Ugbaru; Greek Gobryas), the general who took Babylon for Cyrus and then assisted Cyrus by ruling Mesopotamia (i.e., "the kingdom" of Babylon and not the entire empire) for a short time until he died.

and satraps sought to find *some* charge against Daniel concerning the kingdom; but they could find no charge or fault, because he *was* faithful; nor was there any error or fault found in him. ⁵Then these men said, "We shall not find any charge against this Daniel unless we find *it* against him concerning the law of his God."

⁶So these governors and satraps thronged before the king, and said thus to him: "King Darius, live forever! ⁷All the governors of the kingdom, the administrators and satraps, the counselors and advisors, have consulted together to establish a royal statute and to make a firm decree, that whoever petitions any god or man for thirty days, except you, O king, shall be cast into the den of lions. ⁸Now, O king, establish the decree and sign the writing, so that it cannot be changed, according to the law of the Medes and Persians, which ᵃdoes not alter." ⁹Therefore King Darius signed the written decree.

### Daniel in the Lions' Den

¹⁰Now when Daniel knew that the writing was signed, he went home. And in his upper room, with his windows open toward Jerusalem, he knelt down on his knees three times that day, and prayed and gave thanks before his God, as was his custom since early days.

¹¹Then these men assembled and found Daniel praying and making supplication before his God. ¹²And they went before the king, and spoke concerning the king's decree: "Have you not signed a decree that every man who petitions any god or man within thirty days, except you, O king, shall be cast into the den of lions?"

The king answered and said, "The thing *is* true, according to the law of the Medes and Persians, which ᵃdoes not alter."

¹³So they answered and said before the king, "That Daniel, who is ᵃone of the captives from Judah, does not show due regard

---

6:8 ᵃ Lit. *does not pass away*  6:12 ᵃ Lit. *does not pass away*  6:13 ᵃ Lit. *of the sons of the captivity*

**6:7 whoever petitions any god or man for thirty days, except you.** The plotters against Daniel appealed to the king's ego in order to trap Daniel. **den of lions.** We know that some ancient Near Eastern monarchs kept zoos of exotic animals. In this case the animals would be used for a terrifying form of execution.

**6:8 law of the Medes and Persians, which does not alter.** The notion that human laws are infallible and cannot pass away is contrary to the teaching of Daniel that only God's government is eternal (chap. 2). Human laws are invalid when they conflict with divine law (compare Acts 5:29), because only God possesses total knowledge, wisdom, and power. Notice that the Medes and Persians were already a combined empire with one set of laws (see also Esth. 1:19) before they conquered Babylon.

**6:10 toward Jerusalem.** Daniel prayed toward Jerusalem, the place of the temple and its altar (compare 1 Kin. 8), even though they had been destroyed. Today there is no equivalent holy place of divine-human mediation on earth. Rather, Christians are to pray directly to God in heaven, where Christ, our High Priest, is mediating for us (Heb. 4:14–16). **as was his custom.** Daniel changed nothing about his daily practice of worshiping and praising God, even though he knew that it directly violated the new law. Like his friends when they refused to worship Nebuchadnezzar's image (chap. 3), he ignored the human consequences of putting loyalty to God first.

for you, O king, or for the decree that you have signed, but makes his petition three times a day."

**14**And the king, when he heard *these* words, was greatly displeased with himself, and set *his* heart on Daniel to deliver him; and he ᵃlabored till the going down of the sun to deliver him. **15**Then these men ᵃapproached the king, and said to the king, "Know, O king, that *it is* the law of the Medes and Persians that no decree or statute which the king establishes may be changed."

**16**So the king gave the command, and they brought Daniel and cast *him* into the den of lions. *But* the king spoke, saying to Daniel, "Your God, whom you serve continually, He will deliver you." **17**Then a stone was brought and laid on the mouth of the den, and the king sealed it with his own signet ring and with the signets of his lords, that the purpose concerning Daniel might not be changed.

### Daniel Saved from the Lions

**18**Now the king went to his palace and spent the night fasting; and no ᵃmusicians were brought before him. Also his sleep ᵇwent from him. **19**Then the king arose very early in the morning and went in haste to the den of lions. **20**And when he came to the den, he cried out with a ᵃlamenting voice to Daniel. The king spoke, saying to Daniel, "Daniel, servant of the living God, has your God, whom you serve continually, been able to deliver you from the lions?"

**21**Then Daniel said to the king, "O king, live forever! **22**My God sent His angel and shut the lions' mouths, so that they have not hurt me, because I was found innocent before Him; and also, O king, I have done no wrong before you."

**23**Now the king was exceedingly glad for him, and commanded that they should take Daniel up out of the den. So Daniel was taken up out of the den, and no injury whatever was found on him, because he believed in his God.

---

6:14 ᵃ *strove*   6:15 ᵃ Lit. *thronged before*   6:18 ᵃ Exact meaning unknown   ᵇ Or *fled*   6:20 ᵃ Or *grieved*

**6:14 the king . . . was greatly displeased.** He regretted having bound himself to a commitment that he could not change. Compare Esth. 3:12–15; 8:8 (irrevocable decree to destroy the Jews) and the problem of binding oneself through an oath (Judg. 11:31; 1 Sam. 14:24; Matt. 5:33–37; 14:6–7).

### Darius Honors God

**24**And the king gave the command, and they brought those men who had accused Daniel, and they cast *them* into the den of lions—them, their children, and their wives; and the lions overpowered them, and broke all their bones in pieces before they ever came to the bottom of the den.

**25**Then King Darius wrote:

> To all peoples, nations, and languages that dwell in all the earth:
>
> Peace be multiplied to you.

26 I make a decree that in every dominion of my kingdom *men must* tremble and fear before the God of Daniel.

> For He *is* the living God,
> And steadfast forever;
> His kingdom *is the one* which shall not be destroyed,
> And His dominion *shall endure* to the end.

27 He delivers and rescues,
And He works signs and wonders
In heaven and on earth,
Who has delivered Daniel from the *a*power of the lions.

**28**So this Daniel prospered in the reign of Darius and in the reign of Cyrus the Persian.

### Vision of the Four Beasts

**7** In the first year of Belshazzar king of Babylon, Daniel *a*had a dream and visions of his head *while* on his bed. Then he wrote down the dream, telling *b*the main facts.

**2**Daniel spoke, saying, "I saw in my vision by night, and behold, the four winds of heaven were stirring up the Great Sea. **3**And four great beasts came up from the sea, each different from the other.

---

6:27 *a* Lit. *hand*   7:1 *a* Lit. *saw*   *b* Lit. *the head* or *chief of the words*

**6:24 they brought those men who had accused Daniel.** Unlike those who accused his friends on the basis of accurate information (3:8–12), Daniel's accusers conspired to trick the king into destroying him, even though he was innocent of any wrongdoing, simply because they were jealous. So they were really false accusers who deserved the punishment that they intended for Daniel (compare Deut. 19:16–21). **their children and their wives.** Horrifying as this appears today, destruction of family members was part of the punishment on the guilty men (compare divine retributive justice in Num. 16:27, 31–33). This is partly due to the communal group view of life prevalent at that time and a measure to prevent retaliation.

**6:25 Then King Darius wrote.** Compare proclamations of Nebuchadnezzar regarding the true God (3:29; 4:1–3, 34–37).

**7:1—12:13** These chapters record several visions and explanations of future history, which Daniel himself received.

**7:1 In the first year of Belshazzar.** 550 B.C. Earlier than the events recorded in chaps. 5 and 6.

**7:2 four winds.** This expression can refer to the four directions of the compass (compare 8:8; Jer. 49:36; Zech. 2:6). The winds are stirring up the sea from all directions to create turbulence, presumably representing strife (e.g., Rev. 7:1). **Great Sea.** Represents the turbulent human environment from which the human empires arise (compare Is. 17:12; Rev. 17:15).

**7:3 four great beasts.** These carnivorous animals symbolize powers that reach the top of political strength and authority.

⁴The first *was* like a lion, and had eagle's wings. I watched till its wings were plucked off; and it was lifted up from the earth and made to stand on two feet like a man, and a man's heart was given to it.

⁵"And suddenly another beast, a second, like a bear. It was raised up on one side, and *had* three ribs in its mouth between its teeth. And they said thus to it: 'Arise, devour much flesh!'

⁶"After this I looked, and there was another, like a leopard, which had on its back four wings of a bird. The beast also had four heads, and dominion was given to it.

⁷"After this I saw in the night visions, and behold, a fourth beast, dreadful and terrible, exceedingly strong. It had huge iron teeth; it was devouring, breaking in pieces, and trampling the residue with its feet. It *was* different from all the beasts that *were* before it, and it had ten horns. ⁸I was considering the horns, and there was another horn, a little one, coming up among them, before whom three of the first horns were plucked out by the roots. And there, in this horn, *were* eyes like the eyes of a man, and a mouth speaking ᵃpompous words.

### Vision of the Ancient of Days

⁹ "I watched till thrones were ᵃput in place,
 And the Ancient of Days was seated;
 His garment *was* white as snow,
 And the hair of His head *was* like pure wool.
 His throne *was* a fiery flame,
 Its wheels a burning fire;

---

7:8 ᵃ Lit. *great things*   7:9 ᵃ Or *set up*

**7:4 like a lion, and had eagle's wings.** Just as Babylon was earlier represented by gold, the noblest metal (chap. 2), it is symbolized here by a combination of the most noble carnivorous animal and bird: the lion and the eagle. **a man's heart was given to it.** This depiction of Babylon receiving characteristics of a human being and becoming less like a wild animal of prey could reflect the experience of oppressive Nebuchadnezzar, who became humane and more intelligent when he humbled himself before God (chap. 4). Compare Ezek. 11:19; 36:26.

**7:5 bear . . . raised up on one side . . . three ribs.** This lopsided stance reflects the unequal power between the older Median and younger but stronger Persian sides of the Medo-Persian Empire (compare 8:3, 20). The three ribs seem to represent the bear's victims (such as Lydia, Babylon, and Egypt, which Medo-Persia conquered).

**7:6 leopard . . . four wings of a bird . . . four heads.** Four parts reflect the fact that Alexander the Great's Macedonian/Greek Empire divided into four kingdoms after he died (Macedonia, Pergamum, Egypt, Syria; compare 8:8, 21–22).

**7:7 a fourth beast, dreadful and terrible.** This monster is not like any species of animal that Daniel could identify. Its teeth are of iron, the strong and crushing metal that symbolized the fourth kingdom in chap. 2 (v. 40): Rome. **ten horns.** In symbolic usage in the Bible, horns represent power against enemies (e.g., Deut. 33:17; 1 Sam. 2:1, 10; 2 Sam. 22:3). Here the ten horns are connected to Rome. In Dan. 8 we will see that horns on a symbolic animal represent powers that make up an empire (vv. 3, 20) or parts into which the empire can be split (vv. 8, 21–22). The vast Roman Empire was made of many parts, into which it divided after the city of Rome fell to the barbarians in A.D. 476, as 7:24 predicted (compare 2:41–43).

**7:8 a little one.** As the youngest horn, it starts out small, but grows greater than the other horns (v. 20; compare 8:9—literally, "a horn from smallness"). **before whom three of the first horns were plucked out.** The rise of the little horn to power after the breakup of the Roman Empire involves the fall of three other post-Roman powers (see 7:24). **eyes like the eyes of a man, and a mouth speaking.** Discernment and communication like those of a human being (compare v. 4). **pompous words.** Boastful speech against the Most High God Himself (compare v. 25; for "Most High" as God, compare 3:26; 4:2). The little horn power is not only proud; it has a strong religious agenda and is blasphemous.

**7:9 Ancient of Days.** This unique expression, appearing only in this chapter in the entire Bible, is a title for the Most High God, who lives forever and whose kingdom is everlasting (compare 4:34).

10 A fiery stream issued
And came forth from before Him.
A thousand thousands ministered to Him;
Ten thousand times ten thousand stood before Him.
The ᵃcourt was seated,
And the books were opened.

¹¹"I watched then because of the sound of the ᵃpompous words which the horn was speaking; I watched till the beast was slain, and its body destroyed and given to the burning flame. ¹²As for the rest of the beasts, they had their dominion taken away, yet their lives were prolonged for a season and a time.

13 "I was watching in the night visions,
And behold, *One* like the Son of Man,
Coming with the clouds of heaven!
He came to the Ancient of Days,
And they brought Him near before Him.
14 Then to Him was given dominion and glory and a kingdom,
That all peoples, nations, and languages should serve Him.
His dominion *is* an everlasting dominion,
Which shall not pass away,
And His kingdom *the one*
Which shall not be destroyed.

### Daniel's Visions Interpreted

¹⁵"I, Daniel, was grieved in my spirit ᵃwithin *my* body, and the visions of my head troubled me. ¹⁶I came near to one of those who stood by, and asked him the truth of all this. So he told me and made known to me the interpretation of these things: ¹⁷'Those great beasts, which are four, *are* four ᵃkings *which* arise out of the earth. ¹⁸But the saints of the Most High shall receive the kingdom, and possess the kingdom forever, even forever and ever.'

---

7:10 ᵃ Or *judgment*   7:11 ᵃ Lit. *great*   7:15 ᵃ Lit. *in the midst of its sheath*   7:17 ᵃ Representing their kingdoms, v. 23

**7:10 *The court was seated, and the books were opened.*** This heavenly court, over which God Himself presides, responds to the challenge posed by the "little horn." Books are records that are relevant for determining the verdict and indicate that each case is carefully investigated. The purpose of this judgment (see note on 8:14) is to reveal to the universe that God is just in how He has dealt with and resolved the sin problem. See vv. 22, 26–27 for two more glimpses of this judgment scene. The Bible touches upon books used in judgment in Mal. 3:16–18; Luke 10:20; Rev. 3:5; 20:12; see also Ex. 32:33; Phil. 4:3. For the type of evidence used in the judgment, see Matt. 7:24–27; 16:27; Rom. 2:6, 13; James 2:12. For the judgment in the heavenly sanctuary, see note on Dan. 8:14.

**7:11 *the beast was slain.*** The heavenly judgment condemns the horn, along with the Roman beast from which it has arisen.

**7:12 *dominion taken away, yet their lives were prolonged.*** Peoples who composed the earlier empires remain—as do their cultures, worldviews, and beliefs—even though the empires are gone.

**7:13 *One like the Son of Man.*** A person like a human being (seen again in 8:15; 9:25; 10:5–6; Rev. 1:12–16) approaching the throne of God in heaven to receive God's eternal kingdom on planet Earth (compare Dan. 2:44). This must be Christ, the divine Son of God (Matt. 26:63–64; 27:54; Mark 1:1; compare Dan. 3:25), who also spoke of Himself as the Son of Man and is coming to earth again to set up His eternal kingdom (Matt. 16:27; 19:28). By itself the expression "son of man" can refer to an ordinary human being (Ezek. 2:1, 3, 6, 8), but the person in Dan. 7 is special. When Christ comes to earth a second time, His kingdom will already have been determined in terms of the people who belong to it (Matt. 25:31–46; Rev. 22:11–12). So the judgment in heaven that determines human destinies (Dan. 7:9–14) is before Christ's Second Coming (compare Rev. 14:6–7). Notice that Dan. 7:13 distinguishes between two divine personalities belonging to the holy Trinity: Christ the Son approaches the "Ancient of Days," who must be God the Father (compare Matt. 6:9; 7:21; 28:19).

¹⁹"Then I wished to know the truth about the fourth beast, which was different from all the others, exceedingly dreadful, *with* its teeth of iron and its nails of bronze, *which* devoured, broke in pieces, and trampled the residue with its feet; ²⁰and the ten horns that *were* on its head, and the other *horn* which came up, before which three fell, namely, that horn which had eyes and a mouth which spoke ᵃpompous words, whose appearance *was* greater than his fellows.

²¹"I was watching; and the same horn was making war against the saints, and prevailing against them, ²²until the Ancient of Days came, and a judgment was made *in favor* of the saints of the Most High, and the time came for the saints to possess the kingdom.

²³"Thus he said:

> 'The fourth beast shall be
> A fourth kingdom on earth,
> Which shall be different from all *other* kingdoms,
> And shall devour the whole earth,
> Trample it and break it in pieces.
> 24 The ten horns *are* ten kings
> *Who* shall arise from this kingdom.
> And another shall rise after them;
> He shall be different from the first *ones,*
> And shall subdue three kings.
> 25 He shall speak *pompous* words against the Most High,
> Shall persecuteᵃ the saints of the Most High,
> And shall intend to change times and law.
> Then *the saints* shall be given into his hand
> For a time and times and half a time.
>
> 26 'But the court shall be seated,
> And they shall take away his dominion,
> To consume and destroy *it* forever.

---

7:20 ᵃ Lit. *great things*   7:25 ᵃ Lit. *wear out*

**7:22 judgment was made in favor of the saints of the Most High.** Two opposing human parties are judged: God's faithful people and a rebellious little horn power that attacks them (vv. 21, 25). The verdict is in favor of God's true people, who receive His kingdom as subjects of Christ, but against the "horn." Because the "saints" are also judged, the "books" opened in v. 10 must also record what they have done. This happens before the kingdom is established. For more on this judgment scene, see vv. 9–14, 26–27.

**7:25 times and law.** God's times and laws. It would not be prophetically significant for the little horn power to attempt to change human times and laws, for that is commonly expected in a struggle for worldly dominion. The conflict described here is between earth and heaven. The little horn intends to change God's times and law, most clearly seen in His Ten Commandments. One obvious illustration of God's "times" is His Sabbath. Any attempt by an earthly power to change God's Sabbath is an attempt to change God's law, the heart of which is the Sabbath itself (Ex. 20:8–11; Deut. 5:12–15). The little horn's attempts to change times and laws are not ultimately successful. On the permanency of the Sabbath, see Mark 2:28; Rev. 14:7, 12. **a time and times and half a time.** Also mentioned in Dan. 12:7 and Rev. 12:14. Understood to mean 3 1/2 times or 3 1/2 prophetic years. A prophetic year equals 12 months of 30 prophetic days each, or 360 prophetic days. The 3 1/2 prophetic years, also referred to as 42 months (Rev. 11:2; 13:5) or 1,260 prophetic days (Rev. 11:3; 12:6), correspond to 1,260 years (for the year-day equivalency, see Num. 14:34; Ezek. 4:4–6). Thus, the time predicted for the ruthless reign of the little horn is 1,260 years. Historicist interpreters generally date this from A.D. 538 to 1798 (see Rev. 11:2; 12:6, 14).

**7:26–27 court shall be seated.** Judgment is always for God's people and against His enemies. See Deut. 32:36; Ps. 135:14; Rev. 6:10; 11:15–18; 19:2. The vindication of the people of God (Dan. 7:27) brings with it the condemnation of the little horn (7:11). This scene of judgment (see vv. 9–14, 22) corresponds chronologically to the cleansing of the sanctuary in 8:14.

27 Then the kingdom and dominion,
And the greatness of the kingdoms under the whole heaven,
Shall be given to the people, the saints of the Most High.
His kingdom *is* an everlasting kingdom,
And all dominions shall serve and obey Him.' 

28 "This *is* the end of the [a]account. As for me, Daniel, my thoughts greatly troubled me, and my countenance changed; but I kept the matter in my heart."

## Vision of a Ram and a Goat

**8** In[a] the third year of the reign of King Belshazzar a vision appeared *to* me—to me, Daniel—after the one that appeared to me the first time. 2 I saw in the vision, and it so happened while I was looking, that I *was* in Shushan,[a] the [b]citadel, which *is* in the province of Elam; and I saw in the vision that I was by the River Ulai. 3 Then I lifted my eyes and saw, and there, standing beside the river, was a ram which had two horns, and the two horns *were* high; but one *was* higher than the other, and the higher *one* came up last. 4 I saw the ram pushing westward, northward, and southward, so that no animal could [a]withstand him; nor *was there any* that could deliver from his hand, but he did according to his will and became great.

5 And as I was considering, suddenly a male goat came from the west, across the surface of the whole earth, without touching the ground; and the goat *had* a notable horn between his eyes. 6 Then he came to the ram that had two horns, which I had seen standing beside the river, and ran at him with furious power. 7 And I saw him confronting the ram; he was moved with rage against him, [a]attacked the ram, and broke his two horns. There was no power in the ram to withstand him, but he cast him down to the ground and trampled him; and there was no one that could deliver the ram from his hand.

---

7:28 [a] Lit. *word*  8:1 [a] The Hebrew language resumes in Dan. 8:1.  8:2 [a] Or *Susa*  [b] Or *fortified palace*  8:4 [a] Lit. *stand before him*  8:7 [a] Lit. *struck*

**8:3 a ram which had two horns.** Representing the Medo-Persian Empire, with two unequal horns representing the Median and Persian concentrations of power (v. 20; see note on 7:5). Daniel saw this vision during the reign of Belshazzar (8:1; compare chap. 5), but Babylon was not represented in the vision because its time was almost finished. In this chapter the biblical writer returns to using the Hebrew language (from Aramaic in 2:4—7:28).

**8:4 pushing westward, northward, and southward.** Medo-Persia came from the east (of Palestine) and expanded in these directions.

**8:5 a male goat came from the west.** Symbolizing the Macedonian/Greek Empire, with a single large horn representing its first king (v. 21), namely, Alexander the Great. **without touching the ground.** Depicting the great speed (compare 7:6—leopard with wings) of Alexander's conquests.

**8:7 rage.** The Greeks wanted revenge for what the Medo-Persian Empire had done to them, including the unsuccessful invasion of their territory by Xerxes in 480–479 B.C. (compare 11:2).

⁸Therefore the male goat grew very great; but when he became strong, the large horn was broken, and in place of it four notable ones came up toward the four winds of heaven. ⁹And out of one of them came a little horn which grew exceedingly great toward the south, toward the east, and toward the Glorious *Land*. ¹⁰And it grew up to the host of heaven; and it cast down *some* of the host and *some* of the stars to the ground, and trampled them. ¹¹He even exalted *himself* as high as the Prince of the host; and by him the daily *sacrifices* were taken away, and the place of ᵃ His sanctuary was cast down. ¹²Because of transgression, an army was given over *to the horn* to oppose the daily *sacrifices;* and he cast truth down to the ground. He did *all this* and prospered.

**8:8 *the male goat grew very great.*** Compare 2:39, where the third kingdom of Nebuchadnezzar's image, representing Macedonia/Greece, "shall rule over all the earth." ***when he became strong, the large horn was broken.*** Alexander died at the height of his power in 323 B.C., when he was not quite 33 years old. ***four notable ones came up.*** After a power struggle, Alexander's empire divided into four Greek kingdoms: Antigonid Macedonia, Attalid Pergamum, Ptolemaic Egypt, and Seleucid Syria.

**8:9 *out of one of them.*** The Hebrew syntax makes it clear that this means coming out of one of the four directions, represented by the "four winds of heaven" (see note on 7:2), just mentioned at the end of 8:8. These are the directions toward which Alexander's empire was divided. ***a little horn.*** The next actor on the stage of history, even greater than the empires of Medo-Persia and Alexander the Great. It would become ***exceedingly great.*** The horn is not simply another Greek power or ruler (such as Antiochus IV Epiphanes), but one that takes over all the Greek kingdoms. It is not part of an animal, which would be impossible for a literal horn in real life. However, the vision is

8:11 ᵃ The temple

symbolic. The little horn is the same as the power symbolized in chap. 7. In chap. 8, however, the horn first expands horizontally from the northwest toward the south, the east, and the **Glorious Land** (land of Israel; compare 8:9; 11:16). These are the directions toward which Rome expanded to build its empire, taking over one after another of the Greek kingdoms. Dan. 8:10–12 finds the horn growing vertically against heaven in a religious attack on God, His people, and His truth. Thus the little horn of chap. 8 has both a secular and a religious phase.

**8:10 host of heaven.** Elsewhere this expression can refer to the vast array of heavenly bodies that shine in the sky (Neh. 9:6) or to the Lord's heavenly attendants (Ps. 103:21). Dan. 8 explains that those of the "host of heaven" and "stars" whom the little horn cast down and tramples are the "mighty, and also the holy people" (v. 24). So these are humans on earth who belong to God and therefore are regarded as belonging to heaven (compare 12:3). Because they are on earth, they are vulnerable to attack (compare 7:21, 25; Rev. 13:7).

**8:11 Prince of the host.** The Commander of the armies of heaven is the same being as the Son of Man in 7:13. When Joshua met and worshiped the Commander (same Hebrew word) of the Lord's army, this Being told Joshua to take off his sandals because he was standing at a holy place (Josh. 5:13–15). This is what the Lord commanded Moses at the burning bush (Ex. 3:5). So the Commander is clearly divine, the Lord Himself. Created angels do not allow themselves to be worshiped in this way (Rev. 22:8–9). By exalting himself as high as the Lord, the little horn shares the aspirations of Lucifer, who wants to exalt his throne above the stars of God and make himself "like the Most High" (Is. 14:12–14). **and by him the daily sacrifices were taken away.** Meaning, "removed the regularity/the daily" (compare 11:31; 12:11). The word "sacrifice" is often supplied by translators but is not in the original text. In the context of the earthly sanctuary/temple, the Hebrew term for "regularity" (sometimes referred to as the "continual" or "daily"), applied to a variety or system of regular rituals (lamps, burnt offerings, incense, placing bread) that were performed daily (Ex. 29:38; 30:7–8) or weekly (Lev. 24:8). It designated the daily service of the priest in the court and inside the Holy Place of the tabernacle. It is used here to refer to the mediation of the Prince/Commander of the hosts in the heavenly sanctuary (see Heb. 7:25). The horizontal phase of the little horn represented by the Roman Empire extended beyond the destruction of the Jerusalem temple in A.D. 70. The religious phase of the little horn interfered with the daily ministration of Christ for us in the heavenly temple (see Rev. 13:6). **the place of His sanctuary was cast down.** Compare Rev. 11:2, where the court of God's temple, where His earthly people come to worship, is trampled by the nations/Gentiles for 42 months (= 1,260 days = 3 1/2 years or "times"). This is the period of domination and persecution by the little horn of Dan. 7:25, during which the mediation of Christ in the heavenly temple was obscured through a human system of mediation (see also Rev. 13:6).

**8:12 Because of transgression.** The little horn here casts God's truth to the ground and opposes God's sacred provisions ministered out to sinners by our High Priest through His work of mediation. It also prospers, but for how long? That is the topic of vv. 13–14.

¹³Then I heard a holy one speaking; and *another* holy one said to that certain *one* who was speaking, "How long *will* the vision *be, concerning* the daily *sacrifices* and the transgression ᵃof desolation, the giving of both the sanctuary and the host to be trampled underfoot?"

¹⁴And he said to me, "For two thousand three hundred ᵃdays; then the sanctuary shall be cleansed."

## Gabriel Interprets the Vision

¹⁵Then it happened, when I, Daniel, had seen the vision and was seeking the meaning, that suddenly there stood before me one having the appearance of a man. ¹⁶And I heard a man's voice between *the banks of* the Ulai, who called, and said, "Gabriel, make this *man* understand the vision." ¹⁷So he came near where I stood, and when he came I was afraid and fell on my face; but he said to me, "Understand, son of man, that the vision *refers* to the time of the end."

¹⁸Now, as he was speaking with me, I was in a deep sleep with my face to the ground; but he touched me, and stood me upright. ¹⁹And he said, "Look, I am making known to you what shall happen in the latter time of the indignation; for at the appointed time the end *shall be*. ²⁰The ram which you saw, having the two horns—*they are* the kings of Media and Persia. ²¹And the ᵃmale goat *is* the ᵇkingdom of Greece. The large horn that *is* between its

---

8:13 ᵃ Or *making desolate*   8:14 ᵃ Lit. *evening-mornings*   8:21 ᵃ *shaggy male*   ᵇ Lit. *king*, representing his kingdom, Dan. 7:17, 23

**8:13 How long...?** Here a heavenly being (presumably an angel) asks "until when," emphasizing the moment when the vision of chap. 8 in its totality, including the work of the little horn against the temple and the daily work of the Prince/Commander, will conclude.

**8:14 For two thousand three hundred days.** The Hebrew words translated "days" literally mean "evening mornings." So the time period is 2,300 evenings and mornings. The sequence of evening followed by morning also appears in Gen. 1 with reference to the days of creation (Gen. 1:5, 8, 13, etc.), in Ex. 27:20–21 and Lev. 24:3 for the regular or daily "evening until morning" cycle of burning the lamps on the lampstand in the sanctuary every night, and in Num. 9:15, 21 of God's cloud covering the tabernacle throughout the night. The lamp cycle is closest to the context of Dan. 8, which speaks of regular worship (vv. 11–13) and the sanctuary (vv. 11, 13–14). In these evening-morning passages there is one such sequence during each day of 24 hours. Interpreting the 2,300 evenings and mornings, the Hebrew in v. 26 adds the definite article so as to read "the evenings and the mornings," as if the full expression is "the 2,300 evenings and the 2,300 mornings" (compare Deut. 9:25, in which the definite article in Hebrew is present to mean "the forty days and the forty nights"). This means 2,300 days. If this time were literal, it would be less than 6 1/2 years. Obviously this would not cover the period of the vision from Medo-Persia in B.C. time through the period of domination by the little horn (ending in A.D. 1798; see note on 7:25), which is many centuries. Thus, using historicist principles of prophetic interpretation, the 2,300 days symbolize 2,300 years (compare notes on 7:25; 9:24). Dan. 8 indicates that the period begins during the Medo-Persian Empire while 9:24–25 clarifies that its first segment of 490 years begins with a command to restore and rebuild Jerusalem after the Babylonian exile. We will find (on 9:25) that this command by the Persian king Artaxerxes I went into effect in 457 B.C. Taking 457 B.C. as the beginning of the 2,300 years and remembering that there was no "0" year between B.C. and A.D. time, the end of this period is A.D. 1844. **the sanctuary shall be cleansed.** The verb "cleansed" expresses the idea of the restoration of the order established by God through a work of cleansing and judgment. In the previous verses the activities of the little horn against God and His sanctuary and daily priestly work of Christ in the heavenly sanctuary were described. Now the yearly service, the Day of Atonement (see Lev. 16), is introduced in the vision. The Day of Atonement was a day of judgment in the Israelite temple. The cleansing/reconsecration of the sanctuary mentioned here corresponds to the judgment scene in Dan. 7. This cleansing includes an end-time work of judgment. It is important to remember that Daniel's overall goal is to encourage God's people by clearly foretelling God's deliverance of the righteous and the defeat of His enemies. For more on judgment in the heavenly sanctuary, see 7:9–14.

**8:17 the time of the end.** The same expression also appears in 11:35, 40; 12:4, 9 (compare 8:19) to identify a time near the end of human history, close to Christ's Second Coming (compare 12:1–3), and thus far in the future from Daniel's perspective (compare 8:26).

eyes *is* the first king. ²²As for the broken *horn* and the four that stood up in its place, four kingdoms shall arise out of that nation, but not with its power.

²³ "And in the latter time of their kingdom,
    When the transgressors have reached their fullness,
    A king shall arise,
    Having fierce ᵃfeatures,
    Who understands sinister schemes.

---

**8:23** ᵃ Lit. *countenance*

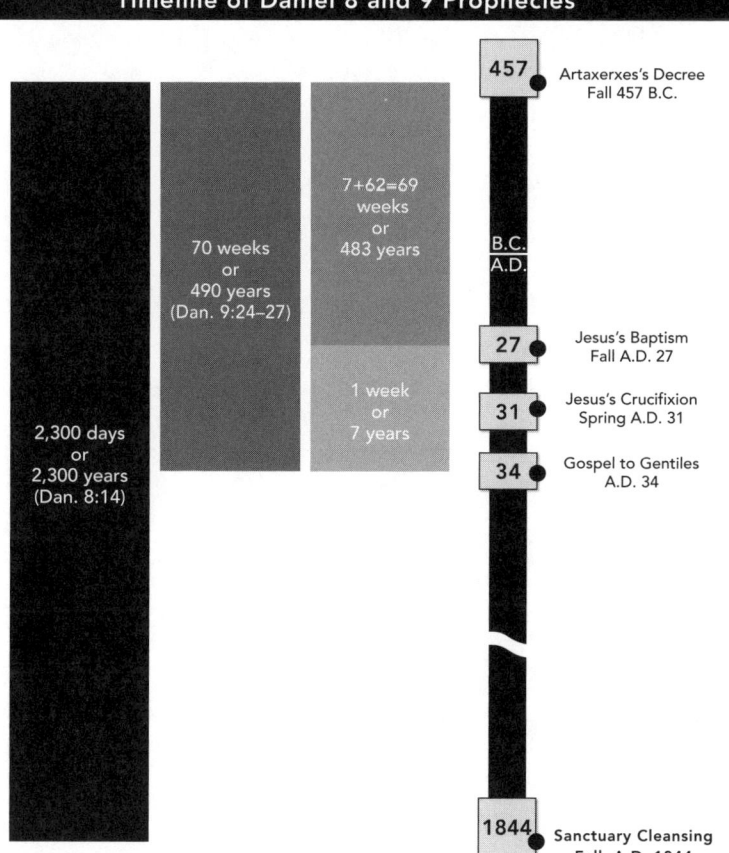

**457 B.C.** Beginning of the 70 weeks (490 years). Marked by the command to restore and rebuild Jerusalem (9:25) issued by the Persian king Artaxerxes I in the seventh year of his reign (Ezra 7:11–26).

**A.D. 27.** End of the 69 weeks (483 years) predicted for the coming of the Messiah the Prince (Dan. 9:25) and beginning of the last week. Fulfilled in the fifteenth year of the reign of Tiberius Caesar when Jesus was baptized and began His ministry (Luke 3:1, 21).

**A.D. 31.** Middle of the last week (Dan. 9:27) of the 70 weeks (490 years). After Christ's 3 1/2 years of earthly ministry, His death confirmed a covenant for the benefit of all.

**A.D. 34.** End of the 70 weeks (490 years). Marked by the martyrdom of Stephen and the related persecution that scattered Christians from Judea, and thus spread the gospel to the Gentiles.

**A.D. 1844.** End of the 2,300 days (2,300 years). Marked the beginning of the cleansing of the heavenly sanctuary and the end-time work of judgment.

²⁴ His power shall be mighty, but not by his own power;
He shall destroy ᵃfearfully,
And shall prosper and thrive;
He shall destroy the mighty, and *also* the holy people.

²⁵ "Through his cunning
He shall cause deceit to prosper under his ᵃrule;
And he shall exalt *himself* in his heart.
He shall destroy many in *their* prosperity.
He shall even rise against the Prince of princes;
But he shall be broken without *human* ᵇmeans.

²⁶ "And the vision of the evenings and mornings
Which was told is true;
Therefore seal up the vision,
For *it refers* to many days *in the future*."

²⁷And I, Daniel, fainted and was sick for days; afterward I arose and went about the king's business. I was ᵃastonished by the vision, but no one understood it.

### Daniel's Prayer for the People

**9** In the first year of Darius the son of Ahasuerus, of the lineage of the Medes, who was made king over the realm of the Chaldeans— ²in the first year of his reign I, Daniel, understood by the books the number of the years *specified* by the word of the LORD through Jeremiah the prophet, that He would accomplish seventy years in the desolations of Jerusalem.

³Then I set my face toward the Lord God to make request by prayer and supplications, with fasting, sackcloth, and ashes. ⁴And I prayed to the LORD my God, and made confession, and said, "O Lord, great and awesome God, who keeps His covenant and mercy with those who love Him, and with those who keep His commandments, ⁵we have sinned and committed iniquity,

---

8:24 ᵃ Or extraordinarily   8:25 ᵃ Lit. hand   ᵇ Lit. hand   8:27 ᵃ amazed

**8:26 seal up the vision.** Compare 12:4. This means that the prophecy of the 2,300 days of 8:14 would not be fully understood until a future time.

**8:27 astonished by the vision, but no one understood it.** The Hebrew word for "vision" here is the one used in v. 26 for the conversation in vv. 13–14 that speaks of the 2,300 days. Daniel realized that the time period was a long one, during which bad things would happen to God's cause in the world and to His people. But because he did not know when the period would begin, he could not know when it would end. He needed additional explanation (see notes on chap. 9).

**9:1 In the first year of Darius.** At the beginning of Medo-Persian rule. **Ahasuerus.** Also called Xerxes, a Median and thus not the same Ahasuerus as the husband of Esther (compare Esth. 1:1). The latter Ahasuerus/Xerxes had a son named Artaxerxes I (see Ezra 4:4–7; Neh. 2:1).

**9:2 Jeremiah . . . seventy years.** Daniel was studying the prophecies of Jeremiah, his older contemporary. Jeremiah recorded God's word that the land of Judah would lie desolate under Babylonian domination for 70 years until Babylon would be punished, and then the Jews could return from exile (Jer. 25:11–12; 29:10). Now Babylon had been punished and a new empire had just taken over (Dan. 5–6). So according to what Jeremiah had said, the end of the 70 years had come and it was time for the Jewish captives to be set free. So Daniel should have been overjoyed.

**9:3 fasting, sackcloth, and ashes.** Rather than rejoicing, Daniel was mourning (compare Esth. 4:1, 3; Ps. 35:13; Is. 58:5; Jer. 6:26). His problem was the vision of Dan. 8, which showed that there would be a long time of difficulty for God's people before the sanctuary would be restored. It is clear that he did not understand the 2,300 days (8:14) to be literal days (less than 6 1/2 years), or he would not have been upset. He naturally would have assumed that the sanctuary was the temple in Jerusalem and associated its justification with restoration after his people would be released from exile. So he would have concluded that because of their sins, God may have decided to postpone the release from Babylonian captivity until far in the future.

**9:4 prayed . . . made confession.** At the end of the covenant blessings and curses in Lev. 26, God had promised that if His exiled people would humble themselves, repent, and confess their sins and those of their ancestors in this way, He would restore them from exile (Lev. 26:40–45).

**9:5 we have sinned.** Not "they have sinned." Daniel was a righteous man (6:3–5) and the Bible does not record any sin that he committed, but he identified himself with his people in this prayer of intercession.

we have done wickedly and rebelled, even by departing from Your precepts and Your judgments. ⁶Neither have we heeded Your servants the prophets, who spoke in Your name to our kings and our princes, to our fathers and all the people of the land. ⁷O Lord, righteousness *belongs* to You, but to us shame of face, as *it is* this day—to the men of Judah, to the inhabitants of Jerusalem and all Israel, those near and those far off in all the countries to which You have driven them, because of the unfaithfulness which they have committed against You.

⁸"O Lord, to us *belongs* shame of face, to our kings, our princes, and our fathers, because we have sinned against You. ⁹To the Lord our God *belong* mercy and forgiveness, though we have rebelled against Him. ¹⁰We have not obeyed the voice of the Lord our God, to walk in His laws, which He set before us by His servants the prophets. ¹¹Yes, all Israel has transgressed Your law, and has departed so as not to obey Your voice; therefore the curse and the oath written in the Law of Moses the servant of God have been poured out on us, because we have sinned against Him. ¹²And He has confirmed His words, which He spoke against us and against our judges who judged us, by bringing upon us a great disaster; for under the whole heaven such has never been done as what has been done to Jerusalem.

¹³"As *it is* written in the Law of Moses, all this disaster has come upon us; yet we have not made our prayer before the Lord our God, that we might turn from our iniquities and understand Your truth. ¹⁴Therefore the Lord has kept the disaster in mind, and brought it upon us; for the Lord our God *is* righteous in all the works which He does, though we have not obeyed His voice. ¹⁵And now, O Lord our God, who brought Your people out of the land of Egypt with a mighty hand, and made Yourself a name, as *it is* this day—we have sinned, we have done wickedly!

¹⁶"O Lord, according to all Your righteousness, I pray, let Your anger and Your fury be turned away from Your city Jerusalem, Your holy mountain; because for our sins, and for the iniquities

DANIEL 9:16

of our fathers, Jerusalem and Your people *are* a reproach to all *those* around us. **¹⁷**Now therefore, our God, hear the prayer of Your servant, and his supplications, and for the Lord's sake ᵃcause Your face to shine on ᵇYour sanctuary, which is desolate. **¹⁸**O my God, incline Your ear and hear; open Your eyes and see our desolations, and the city which is called by Your name; for we do not present our supplications before You because of our righteous deeds, but because of Your great mercies. **¹⁹**O Lord, hear! O Lord, forgive! O Lord, listen and act! Do not delay for Your own sake, my God, for Your city and Your people are called by Your name."

## The Seventy-Weeks Prophecy

**²⁰**Now while I *was* speaking, praying, and confessing my sin and the sin of my people Israel, and presenting my supplication before the Lord my God for the holy mountain of my God, **²¹**yes, while I *was* speaking in prayer, the man Gabriel, whom I had seen in the vision at the beginning, ᵃbeing caused to fly swiftly, reached me about the time of the evening offering. **²²**And he informed *me,* and talked with me, and said, "O Daniel, I have now come forth to give you skill to understand. **²³**At the beginning of your supplications the ᵃcommand went out, and I have come to tell *you,* for you *are* greatly beloved; therefore consider the matter, and understand the vision:

---

9:17 ᵃ Be gracious  ᵇ The temple   9:21 ᵃ Or *being weary with weariness*   9:23 ᵃ Lit. *word*

**9:17–19 Your sanctuary . . . Your city and Your people are called by Your Name.** Like Moses (Ex. 32:11–13; Num. 14:13–19), Daniel interceded with the Lord on behalf of His people by appealing to God's character of mercy and need to preserve His reputation in the world. Daniel was also concerned for their city of Jerusalem and God's sanctuary there on its "holy mountain" (Mount Zion), where God had put His name/identity (compare Deut. 12:5, 11, 21). Concern for the people and sanctuary links Daniel's prayer to his vision of Dan. 8, where the little horn power oppresses the people and acts against the sanctuary.

**9:21 evening offering.** Or "evening grain offering" (2 Kin. 16:15; Ezra 9:4–5). The angel Gabriel (compare Luke 1:19, 26) appeared to Daniel in human form about the time when the last regular sacrifice of the day would have been performed if the temple had been functioning (compare Ex. 29:39–42; Lev. 6:20). This was an appropriate time, as the psalmist said: "Let my prayer be set before You as incense, the lifting up of my hands as the evening sacrifice" (Ps. 141:2).

**9:23 understand the vision.** There is no vision in chap. 9, so this refers to the vision in chap. 8. More precisely, the Hebrew word for "vision" here is the one used in 8:26 for the conversation that speaks of the 2,300 days (8:13–14), which had particularly perplexed Daniel (8:27). Gabriel had come to explain this time element in order to relieve Daniel's distress over the apparent conflict between the 70 years of Jeremiah and the 2,300 days of his own vision.

**24** "Seventy <sup>a</sup>weeks are determined
For your people and for your holy city,
To finish the transgression,
<sup>b</sup>To make an end of sins,
To make reconciliation for iniquity,
To bring in everlasting righteousness,
To seal up vision and prophecy,
And to anoint <sup>c</sup>the Most Holy.

**25** "Know therefore and understand,
*That* from the going forth of the command

---

**9:24 Seventy weeks.** The word for "weeks" means "group of seven," which can be a cycle of days or of years. Here it is obviously years because the events span a much longer period than 490 (70 times 7) literal days. Such matters, for example, as rebuilding Jerusalem could never have been fulfilled in 70 weeks or days (less than 1 1/2 years). Thus it is understood as "weeks of years." For cycles of seven years, see also the sabbatical year periods in Lev. 25. The number "seventy" links this time unit to the 70 years prophesied by Jeremiah (see note on Dan. 9:2). Just as the nation of Judah suffered 70 years of exile as a result of rebellion and sin, it would now have 70 sabbatical year cycles (490 years) at the end of which rebellion will finish and there will be an end of sins. **determined.** This word appears only here in the Hebrew Bible in any form. But in rabbinic writings its basic meaning is to "cut off" from something longer, and thus it can be expressed as "determined," "decreed," "set apart," or "defined." In this verse, both the basic and extended meanings would apply: The 490 years are "cut off" from the longer unit of 2,300 days = years (8:14), and this period of 490 years is "determined" concerning the Jewish people and the holy city of Jerusalem for their benefit. God is the implicit agent of the passive verb, so He does the cutting off or decreeing. Daniel was concerned about the fate of his people, their city, and the temple during the 2,300 days, and here is the answer. **To finish the transgression.** That is, for the purpose of finishing rebellious sin (compare the verb "rebel" from the same root in 1 Kin. 12:19; 2 Kin. 1:1; 3:5).

---

9:24 <sup>a</sup> Lit. *sevens,* and so throughout the chapter   <sup>b</sup> So with Qr., LXX, Syr., Vg.; Kt., Theodotion *To seal up*   <sup>c</sup> The Most Holy Place

For the combination of three terms for moral faults—"transgression," "sin," and "iniquity"/culpability (but with "iniquity" listed first) see also Ex. 34:7; Lev. 16:21. God's cutting off/decreeing the 490 years on behalf of the Jewish people is for Him to fulfill His purposes of (1) clearing up the three kinds of moral evils, which plagued His people throughout their history, and (2) causing three good things: "to bring in everlasting righteousness, to seal up [confirmation of] vision and prophecy, and to anoint the Most Holy." **to anoint the Most Holy.** Consecrating a sanctuary to God for its sacred function (compare Lev. 8:10–12). This consecration would take place centuries after that of the second temple, which was built and dedicated soon after the return from exile (Ezra 6). So this must be consecration of another temple (see note on Dan. 9:25).

**9:25 command to restore and build Jerusalem.** The 490 years (70 times 7) begin from the time of this command, which restores ownership of the city to the Jews as their capital (compare 1 Kin. 20:34; 2 Kin. 14:22). The command was issued by the Persian king Artaxerxes I in the seventh year of his reign (Ezra 7:11–26) and thus went into effect in 457 B.C. Unlike the earlier decrees of Cyrus (537 B.C.; Ezra 1:1–4; 6:3–5) and Darius (520 B.C.; Ezra 6:1–12), that of Artaxerxes explicitly included concern for the city of Jerusalem itself, not just the Jewish people and their temple. Artaxerxes mandated restoration of Jerusalem as the judicial, civil center of the Jewish people. This civil control included the right to rebuild public works (compare 1 Kin. 20:34), which Ezra and his associates began to do before they ran into opposition (Ezra 4:11–16). Later Nehemiah completed this work (Neh. 3–7). Thus the word of God for the restoration of His people from exile, which began to be fulfilled through the commands of Cyrus and Darius, was completed by the decree of Artaxerxes (compare Ezra 6:14). **Messiah the Prince.** The English word "Messiah" is a Hebrew word sometimes translated "Anointed One" or from the Greek "Christ." Kings and priests, especially high priests, were anointed in ancient Israel (Lev. 6:22; 2 Sam. 5:3). The word for "Prince" refers to a leader who could be either a king (1 Sam. 9:16; 13:14) or a priest (1 Chr. 9:10–11; Neh. 11:11; Jer. 20:1). Dan. 9 predicts the ultimate "Anointed One," the "Messiah" whose coming would be associated with putting an end to sin, bringing righteousness, confirming prophecy, and consecrating a sanctuary (v. 24). He is both Priest and King (Ps. 110). According to the NT, this is Jesus Christ. He was anointed by God's Spirit (Luke 4:18), died to forgive our sins and cover us with His righteousness (2 Cor. 5:21), fulfilled prophecy (e.g., Matt. 1:22–23; 2:5–6), and began to serve as our Melchizedek (= "King of Righteousness"), High Priest in God's temple in heaven (Heb. 7–10). **seven weeks and sixty-two weeks.** These 69 weeks of years (see v. 27 regarding the last weeks) are 483 years from 457 B.C. (command of Artaxerxes I), reaching to A.D. 27 (taking into account that there was no zero year between B.C. and A.D. time). In this year, the fifteenth year (according to Jewish reckoning) of the reign of Tiberius Caesar, the Holy Spirit descended upon Jesus at His baptism and He began His ministry (Luke 3). There are many amazing prophecies about Christ in the OT (e.g., Ps. 22; Is. 53), but Dan. 9 is special because it precisely pinpointed the year of His coming more than 500 years in advance. Notice that the first seven weeks of years form a Jubilee cycle of 49 years (Lev. 25:8–10), showing that the 490 years consist of ten Jubilee periods. This suggests that the 490 years are a large-scale Jubilee period, at the end of which freedom (here from sin; Dan. 9:24) would be available on the national level.

To restore and build Jerusalem
Until Messiah the Prince,
*There shall be* seven weeks and sixty-two weeks;
The ªstreet shall be built again, and the ᵇwall,
Even in troublesome times.

26 "And after the sixty-two weeks
Messiah shall ªbe cut off, but not for Himself;
And the people of the prince who is to come
Shall destroy the city and the sanctuary.
The end of it *shall be* with a flood,
And till the end of the war desolations are determined.
27 Then he shall confirm a ªcovenant with many for one week;
But in the middle of the week
He shall bring an end to sacrifice and offering.
And on the wing of abominations shall be one who makes desolate,
Even until the consummation, which is determined,
Is poured out on the ᵇdesolate."

### Vision of the Glorious Man

**10** In the third year of Cyrus king of Persia a message was revealed to Daniel, whose name was called Belteshazzar. The message *was* true, ªbut the appointed time *was* long;

---

9:25 ª Or *open square*  ᵇ Or *moat*   9:26 ª Suffer the death penalty   9:27 ª Or *treaty*  ᵇ Or *desolator*
10:1 ª Or *and of great conflict;*

**9:26 Messiah shall be cut off.** It is remarkable that the Messiah receives this divine penalty for serious sin, which is a kind of permanent death beyond ordinary death of the mortal body (Lev. 20:2–3) and further implies cutting a person off from his family line. Christ suffered the punishment of the "second death" (compare Rev. 2:11; 20:6, 14) for us on the cross in order to save us from it. But because He was innocent and bore blame for everyone else (1 Pet. 2:21–24), He has returned from the ultimate death from which there is no return and sees His offspring (Is. 53:10). **not for Himself.** Showing that the Messiah would be cut off, gaining nothing for Himself. He would be a substitute benefiting others. **the people of the prince who is to come.** After the death of Christ, Imperial Rome under Titus (their "prince") destroyed Jerusalem and its temple in A.D. 70.

**9:27 confirm a covenant with many.** The mention of the last week of the seventy weeks returns the focus to the Messiah and His work, since the time element is only associated with the Messiah (vv. 25–26). Thus, the antecedent for "he" is the Messiah. Christ established a strong covenant for the benefit of everyone by His sacrifice of Himself (Matt. 26:28; compare Jer. 31:31–34). **In the middle of the week.** Meaning the middle of the last seven years (last "week") of the 490 years following 457 B.C. These final seven years began in A.D. 27 (Jesus's baptism). Christ's earthly ministry lasted for the first half of this seven: 3 1/2 years until His death. When He died, the temple veil was torn in two (Matt. 27:51), making obsolete the temple sacrifices that pointed forward to His sacrifice (compare Heb. 10:1). Thus Christ brought **an end to sacrifice and offering.** Then He ascended to heaven and continued to confirm the covenant through the gift of the Holy Spirit in the witness of the apostles (Acts 1–7). In A.D. 34, the end of the final seven years, the Jewish national council rejected the gospel and martyred Stephen (Acts 7). A great persecution arose against the Christians and scattered them (Acts 8:1). Thus, the gospel went to the Gentiles, so that they could become Christians without first becoming Jews (Acts 10–11, 13–15). **one who makes.** The Hebrew text indicates that this person is not the same as the One who brings "an end to sacrifice." The Hebrew word for "abominations" (plural here) refers to idolatry, which is a serious form of rebellion against God (compare Deut. 29:17; 2 Kin. 23:24). The idea of abominations closely followed by desolation refers to the destruction of Jerusalem in A.D. 70 by Imperial Rome (see note on 9:26), which set up idolatrous standards in part of the holy area surrounding the temple that extended outside the city walls during the siege (Matt. 24:15; Mark 13:14). The combination of abomination with desolation also points beyond pagan Rome to the devastation caused by the religious phase of the little horn power in the latter part of the 2,300 years (Dan. 8:11–13—"transgression of desolation"; compare 11:31; 12:11—"abomination of desolation"). The little horn sets up a form of idolatry or false sacrifice to replace the function of the earthly sacrificial system that Christ brought to an end. So after the end of the 490 years, the explanation in 9:27 ties in to the rest of the vision of chap. 8. This reinforces the fact that the 490 years are the first part of the 2,300 years.

**10:1—12:13** Daniel's final great vision traces the story of God's people down to the end of time. The details may seem to be purposefully vague to keep attention focused on the main point of encouraging God's people with the fact that God is leading and that their final salvation is sure.

and he understood the message, and had understanding of the vision. ²In those days I, Daniel, was mourning three full weeks. ³I ate no ᵃpleasant food, no meat or wine came into my mouth, nor did I anoint myself at all, till three whole weeks were fulfilled.

⁴Now on the twenty-fourth day of the first month, as I was by the side of the great river, that *is,* the ᵃTigris, ⁵I lifted my eyes and looked, and behold, a certain man clothed in linen, whose waist *was* girded with gold of Uphaz! ⁶His body *was* like beryl, his face like the appearance of lightning, his eyes like torches of fire, his arms and feet like burnished bronze in color, and the sound of his words like the voice of a multitude.

⁷And I, Daniel, alone saw the vision, for the men who were with me did not see the vision; but a great terror fell upon them, so that they fled to hide themselves. ⁸Therefore I was left alone when I saw this great vision, and no strength remained in me; for my ᵃvigor was turned to ᵇfrailty in me, and I retained no strength. ⁹Yet I heard the sound of his words; and while I heard the sound of his words I was in a deep sleep on my face, with my face to the ground.

### Prophecies Concerning Persia and Greece

¹⁰Suddenly, a hand touched me, which made me tremble on my knees and *on* the palms of my hands. ¹¹And he said to me, "O Daniel, man greatly beloved, understand the words that I speak to you, and stand upright, for I have now been sent to you." While he was speaking this word to me, I stood trembling.

¹²Then he said to me, "Do not fear, Daniel, for from the first day that you set your heart to understand, and to humble yourself before your God, your words were heard; and I have come because of your words. ¹³But the prince of the kingdom of Persia withstood me twenty-one days; and behold, Michael, one of the chief princes, came to help me, for I had been left alone there

10:3 ᵃ *desirable*   10:4 ᵃ Heb. *Hiddekel*   10:8 ᵃ Lit. *splendor*   ᵇ Lit. *ruin*

**10:1 *third year of Cyrus*.** After the writing of at least chap. 1, which ends with the note that "Daniel continued until the first year of King Cyrus."

**10:2 *mourning*.** Daniel was mourning and humbling himself by practicing self-denial (compare v. 12; Lev. 16:29; Ezra 8:21; Ps. 35:13–14) through a partial fast and by abstaining from putting oil as lotion on his skin. He did this because he sought further understanding from God (Dan. 10:12), no doubt regarding the fate of his people (compare v. 14; chap. 9).

**10:5 *man clothed in linen*.** An awesome heavenly being (compare Rev. 1:13–16, describing the glorified Christ) appearing in human form, who came to enlighten Daniel as Gabriel had previously done (Dan. 9:20–27). In Ezek. 9:2–3, 11; 10:2, 6–7 a servant of God, apparently an angel, similarly wears linen.

**10:13 *prince of the kingdom of Persia*.** This could be Cambyses, the son of Cyrus (559–530 B.C.), who may have been resisting God's decision to restore His people. However, the fact that an angel from God would need to fight against this "prince" (v. 20) suggests spiritual warfare against an evil supernatural being (compare Eph. 6:12). If so, there must be demons (evil angels) struggling to influence and control human governments (compare Dan. 10:20—"prince of Greece"; John 12:31—"ruler of this world") in order to counter the purposes of God. The Lord revealed this battle between good and evil near the beginning of rule by the Persians, whose Zoroastrian religion emphasized conflict between good and evil supernatural forces. ***Michael, one of the chief princes*.** Michael (meaning the rhetorical question "Who is like God?") was the name of various men in the OT (e.g., Num. 13:13; 1 Chr. 5:13). But it is also the name of an exalted heavenly person, who is a chief prince (Dan. 10:13). Elsewhere he is the great guardian of Daniel and his people (v. 21; 12:1), "the archangel" who disputed with the devil (Jude 9), and the commander of God's angels, who defeated Satan and his angels and drove them out of heaven (Rev. 12:7–9). So it appears that this Michael is "the Prince of the host," who is Christ (see note on Dan. 8:11). Christ Himself (not a created being) could serve as a messenger (or "angel") from God (see Judg. 6:11 regarding "the angel of the Lord," who is God Himself).

with the kings of Persia. ¹⁴Now I have come to make you understand what will happen to your people in the latter days, for the vision *refers* to *many* days yet *to come.*"

¹⁵When he had spoken such words to me, I ᵃturned my face toward the ground and became speechless. ¹⁶And suddenly, *one* having the likeness of the ᵃsons of men touched my lips; then I opened my mouth and spoke, saying to him who stood before me, "My lord, because of the vision my sorrows have ᵇoverwhelmed me, and I have retained no strength. ¹⁷For how can this servant of my lord talk with you, my lord? As for me, no strength remains in me now, nor is any breath left in me."

¹⁸Then again, *the one* having the likeness of a man touched me and strengthened me. ¹⁹And he said, "O man greatly beloved, fear not! Peace *be* to you; be strong, yes, be strong!"

So when he spoke to me I was strengthened, and said, "Let my lord speak, for you have strengthened me."

²⁰Then he said, "Do you know why I have come to you? And now I must return to fight with the prince of Persia; and when I have gone forth, indeed the prince of Greece will come. ²¹But I will tell you what is noted in the Scripture of Truth. (No one upholds me against these, except Michael your prince.

# 11

"Also in the first year of Darius the Mede, I, *even* I, stood up to confirm and strengthen him.) ²And now I will tell you the truth: Behold, three more kings will arise in Persia, and the fourth shall be far richer than *them* all; by his strength, through his riches, he shall stir up all against the realm of Greece. ³Then a mighty king shall arise, who shall rule with great dominion, and do according to his will. ⁴And when he has arisen, his kingdom shall be broken up and divided toward the four winds of heaven, but not among his posterity nor according to his dominion with which he ruled; for his kingdom shall be uprooted, even for others besides these.

**10:15** ᵃ Lit. *set*   **10:16** ᵃ Theodotion, Vg. *the son;* LXX *a hand*   ᵇ Or *turned upon*

**10:14 *latter days.*** The revelation about to be given (chaps. 11–12) reaches into the distant future (compare note on 2:28), like the prophecies of chaps. 2, 7–9.

**10:16 *touched my lips.*** Compare Is. 6:5–7.

**11:1–45** Daniel 11 is one of the most difficult chapters in the Bible to interpret in detail. Events described are often condensed and vague, which leads to many differing interpretations. There is a majority agreement on the first part of the chapter; but the further one goes into the chapter, the greater becomes the disagreement even among those of the same theological view. While the details are not all clear, the basic message is that God is the Lord of history and, in spite of earthly rulers and their actions, He wins over evil in the end and saves His people. Daniel 11 has many parallels with Daniel 8 and 9.

Interpreters using the continuous historical approach, which these notes do, usually see the chapter beginning with the Persian Empire, which is followed by Greece and in particular with two of the four major divisions the Greek Empire split into after the death of Alexander the Great. These two divisions, the Seleucids ("king of the North," vv. 6–15, headquartered in Syria) and the Ptolemies ("king of the South," vv. 5–15, headquartered in Egypt), interact with each other and the land of Israel. Greece is followed by imperial Rome and then ecclesiastical Rome and finally an apostate religious/political power.

**11:2 *three more kings will arise in Persia.*** Unlike the presentations in chaps. 2, 7, and 8, this prophecy consists of literal language covering future history in much greater detail, with no symbolic representation of powers by an image, animals, or other such items. Daniel received the prophecy during the reign of Cyrus (10:1), and the next three Medo-Persian kings were Cambyses (reigned 530–522 B.C.), Gaumata ("false Bardiya/Smerdis"; 522), and Darius I (522–486). Daniel 11 describes rulers without naming them, so we must identify them by their descriptions. While the first part of the chapter is fairly clear, as things move on it is progressively harder to identify the exact people and events referred to. ***he shall stir up all against the realm of Greece.*** The fourth king after Cyrus was Xerxes I (486–465 B.C.), who mounted a massive invasion of Greece that failed.

**11:3 *Then a mighty king shall arise.*** This is Alexander the Great (336–323 B.C.), whose empire was divided into four Greek kingdoms (v. 4; compare 8:8, 21–22). Notice that once Persia under Xerxes loses to Greece (11:2), chap. 11 skips over all the remaining Persian kings (from 465 B.C. on) and goes directly to the Greek Empire (beginning in 330).

## Warring Kings of North and South

**5** "Also the king of the South shall become strong, as well as *one* of his princes; and he shall gain power over him and have dominion. His dominion *shall be* a great dominion. **6** And at the end of *some* years they shall join forces, for the daughter of the king of the South shall go to the king of the North to make an agreement; but she shall not retain the power of her ᵃauthority, and neither he nor his ᵃauthority shall stand; but she shall be given up, with those who brought her, and with him who begot her, and with him who strengthened her in *those* times. **7** But from a branch of her roots *one* shall arise in his place, who shall come with an army, enter the fortress of the king of the North, and deal with them and prevail. **8** And he shall also carry their gods captive to Egypt, with their ᵃprinces *and* their precious articles of silver and gold; and he shall continue *more* years than the king of the North.

**9** "Also *the king of the North* shall come to the kingdom of the king of the South, but shall return to his own land. **10** However his sons shall stir up strife, and assemble a multitude of great forces; and *one* shall certainly come and overwhelm and pass through; then he shall return to his fortress and stir up strife.

**11** "And the king of the South shall be moved with rage, and go out and fight with him, with the king of the North, who shall muster a great multitude; but the multitude shall be given into the hand of his *enemy*. **12** When he has taken away the multitude, his heart will be ᵃlifted up; and he will cast down tens of thousands, but he will not prevail. **13** For the king of the North will return and muster a multitude greater than the former, and shall certainly come at the end of some years with a great army and much equipment.

**14** "Now in those times many shall rise up against the king of the South. Also, ᵃviolent men of your people shall exalt themselves ᵇin fulfillment of the vision, but they shall fall. **15** So the

---

**11:6** ᵃ Lit. *arm*  **11:8** ᵃ Or *molded images*  **11:12** ᵃ Proud  **11:14** ᵃ Or *robbers*, lit. *sons of breakage*
ᵇ Lit. *to establish*

**11:5 king of the South.** Ptolemy I Soter (305–285 B.C.) of the Ptolemaic Greek dynasty that ruled Egypt, to the south of Palestine. **one of his princes.** Seleucus I Nicator (305–281 B.C.), a general of Alexander who became ruler of Babylon. He was driven out and fled to Egypt, but Ptolemy helped him to regain Babylon. Seleucus greatly expanded his domain and founded the Seleucid dynasty with a capital in Syria, to the north of Palestine. So members of this dynasty were kings of the north in chap. 11. The fact that Seleucus was under Ptolemy for a time explains why he is called "one of his princes."

**11:6 they shall join forces.** Antiochus II Theos (261–246 B.C.) and Ptolemy II Philadelphus (285–246) made an alliance, sealed through the marriage of Antiochus to Berenice, the daughter of Ptolemy II. **king of the North.** Refers to the Seleucus territory located north of Israel. Note that God's people were caught in the middle between North and South.

**11:9 shall come to the kingdom of the king of the South.** In 242 B.C., Seleucus II Callinicus (246–225) tried but failed to get revenge for the invasion of Ptolemy III.

**11:10 his sons shall stir up strife.** The sons of Seleucus II, who waged war against Egypt, were Seleucus III (225–223 B.C.) and Antiochus III the Great (223–187).

**11:13 muster a multitude greater than the former.** Antiochus III recovered and prepared to again attack Egypt, which was now under the control of Ptolemy V (205–180 B.C.), a boy only six years old.

**11:14 many will rise against the king of the South.** During the reign of young Ptolemy V, many Egyptians rebelled against their Greek overlords. The Rosetta Stone records concessions made to them by Ptolemy's regents.

**11:15 the king of the North shall come.** Antiochus III defeated a well-trained Egyptian army and besieged the remaining Egyptian forces at Tyre.

king of the North shall come and build a siege mound, and take a fortified city; and the ᵃforces of the South shall not withstand him. Even his choice troops *shall have* no strength to resist. **¹⁶**But he who comes against him shall do according to his own will, and no one shall stand against him. He shall stand in the Glorious Land with destruction in his ᵃpower.

**¹⁷**"He shall also set his face to enter with the strength of his whole kingdom, and ᵃupright ones with him; thus shall he do. And he shall give him the daughter of women to destroy it; but she shall not stand *with him,* or be for him. **¹⁸**After this he shall turn his face to the coastlands, and shall take many. But a ruler shall bring the reproach against them to an end; and with the reproach removed, he shall turn back on him. **¹⁹**Then he shall turn his face toward the fortress of his own land; but he shall stumble and fall, and not be found.

**²⁰**"There shall arise in his place one who imposes taxes *on* the glorious kingdom; but within a few days he shall be destroyed, but not in anger or in battle. **²¹**And in his place shall arise a vile person, to whom they will not give the honor of royalty; but he shall come in peaceably, and seize the kingdom by intrigue. **²²**With the ᵃforce of a flood they shall be swept away from before him and be broken, and also the prince of the covenant. **²³**And after the league *is made* with him he shall act deceitfully, for he shall come up and become strong with a small *number of* people. **²⁴**He shall enter peaceably, even into the richest places of the province; and he shall do *what* his fathers have not done, nor his forefathers: he shall disperse among them the plunder, ᵃspoil, and riches; and he shall devise his plans against the strongholds, but *only* for a time.

**²⁵**"He shall stir up his power and his courage against the king of the South with a great army. And the king of the South shall be stirred up to battle with a very great and mighty army; but

---

11:15 ᵃ Lit. *arms*   11:16 ᵃ Lit. *hand*   11:17 ᵃ Or *bring equitable terms*   11:22 ᵃ Lit. *arms*   11:24 ᵃ *booty*

**11:16 *He shall stand in the Glorious Land.*** Antiochus III took Palestine (compare vv. 41, 45; 8:9) from Egypt.

**11:17 *he shall give him the daughter of women to destroy it.*** After seizing more territory, Antiochus III sealed a peace treaty with Ptolemy V by giving his daughter, Cleopatra I, in marriage to Ptolemy. Some identify this woman as the famous Cleopatra VII, daughter of Ptolemy XI, who had affairs with the Romans Mark Antony and Julius Caesar, which is incorrect because she was the daughter of the king of the south (Egypt) and her father did not give her in marriage for the political purpose predicted here.

**11:18 *coastlands . . . a ruler.*** The Hebrew word translated "ruler" here can refer to a civil leader (Mic. 3:1, 9) or a military commander (Judg. 11:6, 11). Antiochus III was decisively defeated by the Roman commander Scipio Asiaticus at the Battle of Magnesia in 190 B.C., which forced Antiochus out of Asia Minor.

**11:19 *shall stumble and fall.*** Antiochus III was assassinated in 187 B.C. while attempting to plunder the treasure of a temple, apparently so that he could pay tribute to Rome.

**11:20 *shall arise in his place one.*** The Hebrew text is emphasizing the functional position formerly occupied by another as in Gen. 40:13; 41:13. This Hebrew phrase marks major transitions at the beginnings of this verse and the next. It is not used for normal dynastic succession (vv. 5–19); instead, it appears to signal a transfer to another power: the Roman republic, which defeated Antiochus III (v. 18). ***imposes taxes.*** Or, "one who causes an oppressor to pass through the splendor of the kingdom." In 66 B.C., the Roman senate appointed Pompey to incorporate the area at the east of the Roman Empire. During this process, he took Judea in 63 B.C. and made it a dependent tributary of Rome.

**11:21 *vile person.*** Here is a transition from the Roman republic to another power. Julius Caesar, who did not legitimately inherit "the honor of royalty," played the key role in establishing Imperial Rome.

**11:22 *prince of the covenant.*** Christ, the "prince of the covenant" (see notes on 9:25–27) died during the reign of the Roman emperor Tiberius.

**11:23 *a small number of people.*** This would not fit Imperial Rome itself, which was already exceedingly powerful by the time Christ was crucified (v. 22). The Church of Rome made an alliance with Imperial Rome during the reign of the emperor Constantine.

**11:25 *great army.*** The Church of Rome called the Christian nations of Europe to fight the "Crusades" (A.D. 1095–1291) against the Islamic Empire (caliphate; vv. 25–30).

he shall not stand, for they shall devise plans against him. **²⁶**Yes, those who eat of the portion of his delicacies shall destroy him; his army shall ᵃbe swept away, and many shall fall down slain. **²⁷**Both these kings' hearts *shall be* bent on evil, and they shall speak lies at the same table; but it shall not prosper, for the end *will* still *be* at the appointed time. **²⁸**While returning to his land with great riches, his heart shall be *moved* against the holy covenant; so he shall do *damage* and return to his own land.

### The Northern King's Blasphemies

**²⁹**"At the appointed time he shall return and go toward the south; but it shall not be like the former or the latter. **³⁰**For ships from ᵃCyprus shall come against him; therefore he shall be grieved, and return in rage against the holy covenant, and do *damage*.

"So he shall return and show regard for those who forsake the holy covenant. **³¹**And ᵃforces shall be mustered by him, and they shall defile the sanctuary fortress; then they shall take away the daily *sacrifices,* and place *there* the abomination of desolation. **³²**Those who do wickedly against the covenant he shall ᵃcorrupt with flattery; but the people who know their God shall be strong, and carry out *great exploits.* **³³**And those of the people who understand shall instruct many; yet *for many* days they shall fall by sword and flame, by captivity and plundering. **³⁴**Now when they fall, they shall be aided with a little help; but many shall join with them by ᵃintrigue. **³⁵**And *some* of those of understanding shall fall, to refine them, purify *them,* and make *them* white, *until* the time of the end; because *it is* still for the appointed time.

**³⁶**"Then the king shall do according to his own will: he shall exalt and magnify himself above every god, shall speak blasphemies against the God of gods, and shall prosper till the wrath has been accomplished; for what has been determined shall be done. **³⁷**He shall regard neither the ᵃGod of his fathers nor the desire

---

**11:26** ᵃ Or *overflow*   **11:30** ᵃ Heb. *Kittim,* western lands, especially Cyprus   **11:31** ᵃ Lit. *arms*
**11:32** ᵃ *pollute*   **11:34** ᵃ Or *slipperiness, flattery*   **11:37** ᵃ Or *gods*

**11:31 take away the daily.** These words closely parallel those in 8:11–13. Notice that chap. 11 first focuses on political aspects of the Church of Rome (vv. 23–30) and then concentrates on its religious activities (vv. 31–39), some of which began before the Crusades (12:11).

**11:36 exalt and magnify himself above every god.** Compare parallel prophecies of arrogant blasphemy by the Church of Rome in 7:8, 25; 8:11, 25; 2 Thess. 2:3–4; Rev. 13:1–6.

of women, nor regard any god; for he shall exalt himself above *them* all. **38**But in their place he shall honor a god of fortresses; and a god which his fathers did not know he shall honor with gold and silver, with precious stones and pleasant things. **39**Thus he shall act against the strongest fortresses with a foreign god, which he shall acknowledge, *and* advance *its* glory; and he shall cause them to rule over many, and divide the land for ᵃgain.

### The Northern King's Conquests

**40**"At the time of the end the king of the South shall attack him; and the king of the North shall come against him like a whirlwind, with chariots, horsemen, and with many ships; and he shall enter the countries, overwhelm *them,* and pass through. **41**He shall also enter the Glorious Land, and many *countries* shall be overthrown; but these shall escape from his hand: Edom, Moab, and the ᵃprominent people of Ammon. **42**He shall stretch out his hand against the countries, and the land of Egypt shall not escape. **43**He shall have power over the treasures of gold and silver, and over all the precious things of Egypt; also the Libyans and Ethiopians *shall follow* at his heels. **44**But news from the east and the north shall trouble him; therefore he shall go out with great fury to destroy and annihilate many. **45**And he shall plant the tents of his palace between the seas and the glorious holy mountain; yet he shall come to his end, and no one will help him.

### Prophecy of the End Time

**12** "At that time Michael shall stand up,
The great prince who stands *watch* over the sons of your people;

---

11:39 ᵃ *profit*   11:41 ᵃ Lit. *chief of the sons of Ammon*

**11:40 At the time of the end.** Vv. 40–45 depict the attempts of the end-time enemy of God to establish lasting control over the whole world. Such activity (8:17, 19; 11:35; 12:4, 9) happens shortly before Christ's Second Coming, after the Church of Rome revives following the end of its 1,260 years of domination (see notes on 7:25; 8:17; and Rev. 13:3). While the events predicted in Dan. 11:1–39 have happened in the past from our perspective, fulfillment of vv. 40–45 has not been completed. Historicist interpreters now generally agree that the "king of the North" here continues to represent the Church of Rome. However, there are two main views regarding the identity of the "king of the South" ruling Egypt and a number of other countries (vv. 40–43). Historicist scholars often interpret this power as atheism, based on (1) the idea that entities during the Christian era predicted by a symbolic apocalyptic prophecy must be spiritual/religious, and (2) "Egypt" in Rev. 11:8 is sometimes interpreted as a symbolic description of atheistic France during the French Revolution. However, some scholars interpret this power to be a continuation of the religious-political power that fought the Crusades against the religious-political power of the Church of Rome (vv. 25–30), considering that (1) Daniel 11 is not symbolic prophecy, but basically literal, and (2) "Egypt" in Rev. 11:8 differs in usage from that in Dan. 11. The precise future events on earth are known only to God before they actually take place. Prophetic predictions are given in the Bible not to make people speculate about the future, but rather to build faith after those things have come to pass (see Jesus's words in John 14:29).

**11:41 Edom, Moab, and . . . Ammon.** Three neighboring nations whose territories were located to the east and south of the land of Judah in what is now the country of Jordan. They were related to Israel through the patriarchal family ties. These ancient names refer to their end-time equivalents.

**11:45 the glorious holy mountain.** This expression designates the Temple Mount located in the city of Jerusalem. Compare vv. 16 and 41, where "the Glorious Land" is the land of Israel, and see Ps. 48:1. **shall come to his end.** This is because of the rise of Michael (12:1). Compare 8:25, speaking of the same power: "But he shall be broken without human means." The great rebel against God is destroyed at Christ's Second Coming (2 Thess. 2:8; Rev. 19:19–20).

**12:1 Michael shall stand up.** Michael (probably Christ; see note on 10:13), the heavenly guardian of God's people, stands up when the apostate power and its allies are intent on destroying many. This implies that their target is God's people. Shortly before Christ's Second Coming, God's end-time people will threaten the powers that be (compare Rev. 13) by proclaiming a gospel message of allegiance to the Creator God and accountability to Him during the time of His judgment (Rev. 14:6–12). **time of trouble.** Compare Rev. 15–16. **written in the book.** Christ's "Book of Life," recording the names of those who receive eternal life (compare Rev. 3:5; 13:8; 17:8; 20:12, 15; 21:27). By the time Michael stands up, the judgment process of decision involving books/records (Dan. 7:10) has ended and all that remains is to administer positive and negative verdicts (compare 12:2; Matt. 25:31–46; Rev. 22:11–12).

> And there shall be a time of trouble,
> Such as never was since there was a nation,
> *Even* to that time.
> And at that time your people shall be delivered,
> Every one who is found written in the book.
> 2 And many of those who sleep in the dust of the earth shall awake,
> Some to everlasting life,
> Some to shame *and* everlasting [a]contempt.
> 3 Those who are wise shall shine
> Like the brightness of the firmament,
> And those who turn many to righteousness
> Like the stars forever and ever.

**4**"But you, Daniel, shut up the words, and seal the book until the time of the end; many shall run to and fro, and knowledge shall increase."

**5**Then I, Daniel, looked; and there stood two others, one on this riverbank and the other on that riverbank. **6**And *one* said to the man clothed in linen, who *was* above the waters of the river, "How long shall the fulfillment of these wonders *be?*"

**7**Then I heard the man clothed in linen, who *was* above the waters of the river, when he held up his right hand and his left hand to heaven, and swore by Him who lives forever, that *it shall be* for a time, times, and half *a time;* and when the power of the holy people has been completely shattered, all these *things* shall be finished.

**8**Although I heard, I did not understand. Then I said, "My lord, what *shall be* the end of these *things?*"

**9**And he said, "Go *your way,* Daniel, for the words *are* closed up and sealed till the time of the end. **10**Many shall be purified, made white, and refined, but the wicked shall do wickedly; and none of the wicked shall understand, but the wise shall understand.

**12:2** [a] Lit. *abhorrence*

**12:2 *those who sleep in the dust of the earth shall awake.*** This is the resurrection at Christ's Second Coming (1 Thess. 4:15–17; but see Rev. 1:7), which further indicates that Michael is Christ. For more on the resurrection in the OT, see Job 19:25–26; Is. 26:19. In the NT, see Acts 24:15; 1 Cor. 15:51–55; 1 Thess. 4:13–18. On death described as a sleep, see John 11:11–14; Acts 7:60; 1 Thess. 4:13–14.

**12:4 *shut up the words, seal the book until the time of the end.*** Daniel mentions that only two parts of his prophecy would be sealed until the time of the end: (1) the 1,260-day prophecy of 12:7, 9; 7:25 and (2) the 2,300-day prophecy of 8:26, 14. Both of these prophecies are featured in Rev. 11–14 after the little book of Rev. 10 is opened. ***shall run to and fro.*** Many will search the Scriptures diligently in order to understand the prophecies of Daniel. ***knowledge shall increase.*** In the end time there would be increased knowledge so that the prophecy could be understood.

**12:7 *a time, times, and half a time.*** 3½ years, 42 months, or 1,260 days (see note on 7:25).

¹¹"And from the time *that* the daily *sacrifice* is taken away, and the abomination of desolation is set up, *there shall be* one thousand two hundred and ninety days. ¹²Blessed *is* he who waits, and comes to the one thousand three hundred and thirty-five days.

¹³"But you, go *your way* till the end; for you shall rest, and will arise to your inheritance at the end of the days."

**12:11–12** The two time periods mentioned here are related to but slightly different from the time period in 7:25 and 12:7, indicating that they begin, end, and overlap in approximately the same era.

**12:13 *will arise to your inheritance.*** Daniel was given the wonderful assurance that he would enjoy ultimate salvation (compare 2 Tim. 4:7–8).

# REVELATION

### Introduction and Benediction

**1** The Revelation of Jesus Christ, which God gave Him to show His servants—things which must <sup>a</sup>shortly take place. And He sent and signified *it* by His angel to His servant John, ²who bore witness to the word of God, and to the testimony of Jesus Christ, to all things that he saw. ³Blessed *is* he who reads and those who hear the words of this prophecy, and keep those things which are written in it; for the time *is* near.

### Greeting the Seven Churches

⁴John, to the seven churches which are in Asia:

Grace to you and peace from Him who is and who was and who is to come, and from the seven Spirits who are before His throne, ⁵and from Jesus Christ, the faithful witness, the firstborn from the dead, and the ruler over the kings of the earth.

To Him who <sup>a</sup>loved us and washed us from our sins in His own blood, ⁶and has made us <sup>a</sup>kings and priests to His God and Father, to Him *be* glory and dominion forever and ever. Amen.

---

1:1 <sup>a</sup> *quickly* or *swiftly*    1:5 <sup>a</sup> NU *loves us and freed;* M *loves us and washed*    1:6 <sup>a</sup> NU, M *a kingdom*

**1:1** *of Jesus Christ.* Can mean the message came from Jesus, is about Him, or both. *must shortly take place.* Allusion to Dan. 2:28, 45. Revelation is modeled on the style and content of Dan. 2: sequences of history in symbolic format that began to be fulfilled in John's day just as Daniel's began in his (Dan. 2:36–38). *signified it.* The vision employs symbolic language about the future that readers then and now both understand (John 21:19; Acts 11:28). *John.* While the Bible does not tell us who this "John" was, most early historical sources identify him with the John of the Gospels, brother of James, son of Zebedee, a disciple of Jesus (Matt. 4:21–22; 17:1; Mark 3:17; 10:35–41; Luke 9:28, 54; 22:8). This identification is supported by the evidence of Revelation itself, which contains many parallels of language with the Gospel of John.

**1:2** *the word of God.* Probably the OT here, though it should be noted that John, in his Gospel, emphasized that Jesus Himself is the Word (John 1:1–3). *the testimony of Jesus Christ.* John's experience with Jesus as recorded in his Gospel and here in Revelation.

**1:3** *Blessed.* The first of seven "beatitudes" in Revelation (see also 14:13; 16:15; 19:9; 20:6; 22:7, 14). The number seven is central to the book and symbolizes perfection/completion (as the week is completed or perfected on the seventh day) and thus is a number to be associated with a revelation of Jesus. *he who reads.* Revelation was intended to be read aloud in worship. *the time is near.* See note on 1:1.

**1:4–8** A plain-language summary of the major themes of the book: the Godhead, the roles and actions of Jesus, and His Second Coming.

**1:4–5** *seven churches.* John was the spiritual leader of the churches in western Asia minor, and the cities where these churches were located form a rough circle with about a 50-mile (80 km) radius across western Turkey. They are listed in Revelation in clockwise order beginning with Ephesus in the southwest. The vision of Revelation came at a time when these churches began to suffer persecution toward the end of Emperor Domitian's reign (A.D. 95). *Asia.* A Roman province located in western Turkey. *Grace.* Greek greeting. *peace.* Hebrew greeting. *Him who is . . . and who is to come.* A rough paraphrase of God's name as found in Ex. 3:14–15. *seven Spirits.* A reference to the Holy Spirit in the fullness or perfection (hence "seven") of His ministry. Note that Rev. 1:4–5 mentions each member of the Godhead or Trinity—the Father (as "Him who is and who was and who is to come"), the Spirit ("the seven Spirits"), and Jesus Christ—thus, the messages to the churches can be understood as coming from God in all roles. See 4:2, 5; 5:5–6; 22:16–21.

**1:5–6** *the faithful witness . . . kings of the earth.* Jesus's qualifications to rule over us: His witness to God through His life and death, His resurrection, and His universal reign. *To Him who.* Begins a list of Jesus's actions in our behalf: He loves us, died for us, and raised us to the highest possible status. *kings and priests.* See Ex. 19:6; 1 Pet. 2:9. To govern (Gen. 1:28) in the political realm and represent God to those we serve (Ezek. 44:23–24) in the religious realm.

⁷Behold, He is coming with clouds, and every eye will see Him, even they who pierced Him. And all the tribes of the earth will mourn because of Him. Even so, Amen.

⁸"I am the Alpha and the Omega, ᵃ*the* Beginning and *the* End," says the ᵇLord, "who is and who was and who is to come, the Almighty."

### Vision of the Son of Man

⁹I, John, ᵃboth your brother and companion in the tribulation and kingdom and patience of Jesus Christ, was on the island that is called Patmos for the word of God and for the testimony of Jesus Christ. ¹⁰I was in the Spirit on the Lord's Day, and I heard behind me a loud voice, as of a trumpet, ¹¹saying, ᵃ"I am the Alpha and the Omega, the First and the Last," and, "What you see, write in a book and send *it* to the seven churches ᵇwhich are in Asia: to Ephesus, to Smyrna, to Pergamos, to Thyatira, to Sardis, to Philadelphia, and to Laodicea."

¹²Then I turned to see the voice that spoke with me. And having turned I saw seven golden lampstands, ¹³and in the midst of the seven lampstands *One* like the Son of Man, clothed with a garment down to the feet and girded about the chest with a golden band. ¹⁴His head and hair *were* white like wool, as white as snow, and His eyes like a flame of fire; ¹⁵His feet *were* like fine brass, as if refined in a furnace, and His voice as the sound of many waters; ¹⁶He had in His right hand seven stars, out of His mouth went a sharp two-edged sword, and His countenance *was* like the sun shining in its strength. ¹⁷And when I saw Him, I fell at His feet

---

**1:8** ᵃ NU, M omit *the Beginning and the End*  ᵇ NU, M *Lord God*  **1:9** ᵃ NU, M omit *both*  **1:11** ᵃ NU, M omit *"I am the Alpha and the Omega, the First and the Last," and,*  ᵇ NU, M omit *which are in Asia*

**1:7 coming with clouds.** Literary allusion to Dan. 7:13. See also Matt. 24:30; 26:64; Mark 13:26; 14:62. **every eye.** The Second Coming of Jesus will be a universally visible event, unlike His first one. For more on the manner of Christ's Second Coming, see Matt. 25:31; 1 Thess. 4:16–17; 2 Thess. 1:8. **pierced Him.** Allusion to Zech. 12:10 and Jesus's crucifixion (John 19:34). This language suggests a special resurrection of select individuals just before Jesus's return, especially those who crucified Him (Matt. 26:62).

**1:8 the Alpha and the Omega.** First and last letters of the Greek alphabet. Also applied to Jesus in 22:13. God is in full control of the past, the present, and the future.

**1:9 tribulation.** John and his readers have suffered for the gospel. Suffering is never pleasant, but it can produce patience. **Patmos.** An island in the Aegean Sea off the coast of Asia Minor, modern-day Turkey (Rev. 1:9). This is where John received the visions of Revelation while being in exile for his faith in Jesus. **for the word of God.** Implies the gospel is the reason he is on the island (in exile). **testimony.** Translated "witness" in v. 5.

**1:10 in the Spirit.** The first of four references and probably indicates the onset of a vision (see also 4:2; 17:3; 21:10). **the Lord's Day.** While later some Christians came to associate the Lord's Day with Sunday, in the Bible the Lord's Day is the seventh-day Sabbath. See also Is. 58:13–14; Mark 2:27–28.

**1:11 What you see.** Precedes the vision of Christ (vv. 12–18). **seven churches.** This is the first listing of the cities in which the seven churches are found.

**1:12 seven golden lampstands.** Allusion to the lampstand in the OT sanctuary (Ex. 25:31–40; 27:20–21; 37:17–24; 1 Kin. 7:49). But this scene is not in the heavenly sanctuary; the seven lampstands represent the seven churches on earth (Rev. 1:20, see also 1 Cor. 3:16–17; Eph. 2:19–22; 1 Pet. 2:4–6).

**1:13–16** This has numerous similarities to the descriptions in Dan. 7:9–14; 10:5–7. Various characteristics of Christ in this vision are related to the individual churches in Rev. 2–3. Each church receives a unique picture of Jesus.

**1:13 Son of Man.** Jesus's favorite self-designation (see Mark 2:28; Luke 19:10) and an allusion to Dan. 7:13. The glorified Jesus is dressed like the OT high priest (see Ex. 28:1–30).

**1:14–17** Throughout this passage Jesus is repeatedly described in language that is reserved for God in the Old Testament.

**1:16 seven stars.** See v. 20. **two-edged sword.** Represents the judging power of God's word (Heb. 4:12–13).

**1:17 fell . . . as dead.** Just as Daniel did (Dan. 8:17; 10:8–9, 15–16). **the First and the Last.** Applied to God in the OT (Is. 44:6; 48:12).

as dead. But He laid His right hand on me, saying ªto me, "Do not be afraid; I am the First and the Last. **<sup>18</sup>**I *am* He who lives, and was dead, and behold, I am alive forevermore. Amen. And I have the keys of ªHades and of Death. **<sup>19</sup>**ªWrite the things which you have seen, and the things which are, and the things which will take place after this. **<sup>20</sup>**The ªmystery of the seven stars which you saw in My right hand, and the seven golden lampstands: The seven stars are the ᵇangels of the seven churches, and the seven lampstands ᶜwhich you saw are the seven churches.

## The Loveless Church

**2** "To the ªangel of the church of Ephesus write,

'These things says He who holds the seven stars in His right hand, who walks in the midst of the seven golden lampstands: **<sup>2</sup>**"I know your works, your labor, your ªpatience, and that you cannot ᵇbear those who are evil. And you have tested those who say they are apostles and are not, and have found them liars; **<sup>3</sup>**and you have persevered and have patience, and have labored for My name's sake and have not become weary. **<sup>4</sup>**Nevertheless I have *this* against you, that you have left your first love. **<sup>5</sup>**Remember therefore from where you have fallen; repent and do the first works, or else I will come to you quickly and remove your lampstand from its place—unless you repent. **<sup>6</sup>**But this you have, that you hate the deeds of the Nicolaitans, which I also hate.

**<sup>7</sup>**"He who has an ear, let him hear what the Spirit says to the churches. To him who overcomes I will give to eat from the tree of life, which is in the midst of the Paradise of God." '

## The Persecuted Church

**<sup>8</sup>**"And to the ªangel of the church in Smyrna write,

'These things says the First and the Last, who was dead, and came to life: **<sup>9</sup>**"I know your works, tribulation, and poverty (but

---

1:17 ª NU, M omit *to me*   1:18 ª Lit. *Unseen;* the unseen realm   1:19 ª NU, M *Therefore, write*
1:20 ª *hidden truth*   ᵇ Or *messengers*   ᶜ NU, M omit *which you saw*   2:1 ª Or *messenger*
2:2 ª *perseverance*   ᵇ *endure*   2:8 ª Or *messenger*

**1:18 Hades.** The Greek word for the grave, meaning the same as the commonly used Hebrew word in the OT that designated the same place (see Job 17:13; Song 8:6).

**1:19 Write . . . have seen.** See v. 11. John is reminded, in the midst of the vision, to write what he is seeing, because the vision continues.

**1:20 angels.** The word in Greek means "messenger." Thus, it could here mean the respective human leaders of those churches who were to deliver John's message. See Rev. 2:1, 8, for example.

**2:1—3:22** These seven messages are in the form of ancient letters. Addressed to seven churches in Roman Asia, the messages have universal value (2:7, 11) and also offer a symbolic preview of major turns in the future of the Christian church. The promises "to him who overcomes" increase in number and value through the progression of these letters (2:7, 11, 17, 27–28).

**2:1 Ephesus.** Most important city of Roman Asia, a great seaport. Paul spent three years there (Acts 20:31). May represent the relative purity of the church in the first century. **seven stars . . . lampstands.** God guides His messengers and is with His churches (Rev. 1:12, 16, 20).

**2:2 I know your works.** Repeated in each letter. Jesus has full understanding of each situation. **you have tested.** Believers need to test those who claim to speak for God (1 John 4:1).

**2:4 first love.** Compare Eph. 1:15–16; 6:24. Love is the first thing to slip when one turns away from God.

**2:5 remove your lampstand.** The Bible does not teach "once saved always saved." Faith and love must be continually nurtured.

**2:6 Nicolaitans.** A group within the church who compromised with the erroneous popular religious culture. See vv. 14–15. To keep its message and practice clear, a church sometimes has to discipline members.

**2:7 let him hear.** The messages to all seven churches can apply to every reader. **overcomes.** Perseveres in faith and obedience to Christ. **tree of life.** Allusion to the garden of Eden (Gen. 2:9; 3:22, 24). The original conditions will be restored when sin is removed from the earth (see Rev. 22:2).

**2:8 Smyrna.** Important seaport 30 miles (50 km) north of Ephesus with a large Jewish population in John's day. It may represent the persecuted church of the second and third centuries as it is the place where Polycarp was burned alive. Along with the church of Philadelphia (3:7–13), it received no correction from Jesus. **the First . . . came to life.** God is in control from beginning to end, even if that end is death (see 1:17–18).

**2:9 tribulation.** This church was suffering persecution. **say they are Jews.** See Rom. 2:28–29. **synagogue of Satan.** These harsh words suggest that the sizable Jewish population may have led a persecution of Christians in Smyrna.

you are rich); and *I know* the blasphemy of those who say they are Jews and are not, but *are* a ᵃsynagogue of Satan. ¹⁰Do not fear any of those things which you are about to suffer. Indeed, the devil is about to throw *some* of you into prison, that you may be tested, and you will have tribulation ten days. Be faithful until death, and I will give you the crown of life.

¹¹"He who has an ear, let him hear what the Spirit says to the churches. He who overcomes shall not be hurt by the second death." '

### The Compromising Church

¹²"And to the ᵃangel of the church in Pergamos write,

'These things says He who has the sharp two-edged sword: ¹³"I know your works, and where you dwell, where Satan's throne *is*. And you hold fast to My name, and did not deny My faith even in the days in which Antipas *was* My faithful martyr, who was killed among you, where Satan dwells. ¹⁴But I have a few things against you, because you have there those who hold the doctrine of Balaam, who taught Balak to put a stumbling block before the children of Israel, to eat things sacrificed to idols, and to commit sexual immorality. ¹⁵Thus you also have those who hold the doctrine of the Nicolaitans, ᵃwhich thing I hate. ¹⁶Repent, or else I will come to you quickly and will fight against them with the sword of My mouth.

¹⁷"He who has an ear, let him hear what the Spirit says to the churches. To him who overcomes I will give some of the hidden manna to eat. And I will give him a white stone, and on the stone a new name written which no one knows except him who receives *it*." '

### The Corrupt Church

¹⁸"And to the ᵃangel of the church in Thyatira write,

'These things says the Son of God, who has eyes like a flame of fire, and His feet like fine brass: ¹⁹"I know your works, love,

---

**2:9** ᵃ *congregation*  **2:12** ᵃ Or *messenger*  **2:15** ᵃ NU, M *likewise.*  **2:18** ᵃ Or *messenger*

**2:10 tribulation ten days.** See note on 11:2. Read as a preview of history, this could refer to the ten-year (Num. 14:34; Ezek. 4:6) persecution of Christians by Emperor Diocletian, A.D. 303–313. ***crown.*** Not the royal crown, but the garland awarded to the winner in athletic contests.

**2:11 second death.** Although Christians might die, they have ultimate hope (see note on 20:14).

**2:12 Pergamos.** 50 miles (80 km) north of Smyrna, built on a cone-shaped, 1,000-foot (300 m) hill. May represent the church's compromises with the world, since it was known to adopt the latest popular cultures in the centuries following Diocletian's persecutions of A.D. 303–313. ***two-edged sword.*** God's word is how His people can know right from wrong (see 1:16).

**2:13 Satan's throne.** Pergamos was famous for its Great Altar of Zeus. This expression probably refers to that altar, which is now located in a Berlin museum.

**2:14 Balaam.** Allusions to the OT narrative in Num. 22–25. ***to eat things . . . immorality.*** Traditional Roman religion centered on idolatry and sexual immorality. Active citizens of the city were expected to participate in these pagan rituals. Christians were, therefore, tempted to compromise in these areas (see on 1 Cor. 8).

**2:15 Nicolaitans.** Jesus identified these members of the church as the Christian counterparts of Balaam because of their immoral influence.

**2:17 hidden manna.** See Ex. 16:1–36. A portion of manna was "hidden" in front of the ark of the covenant as a memorial. ***white stone.*** In ancient times, a judge gave a white stone to indicate his decision of legal acquittal or pardon. He presented a black stone if the defendant was guilty. ***name.*** See note on Rev. 14:1.

**2:18 Thyatira.** A city 30 miles (50 km) southeast of Pergamos. Thyatira may represent the apostasy of the medieval church, but also the progress of the Reformation (v. 19), since it was a city often captured, destroyed, and rebuilt. ***eyes . . . fine brass.*** God can purify and bring salvation to any willing one (see 1:14–15).

**2:19 the last are more than the first.** Although the condition of this church was grave, it was improving.

ᵃservice, faith, and your ᵇpatience; and *as* for your works, the last *are* more than the first. ²⁰Nevertheless I have ᵃa few things against you, because you allow ᵇthat woman Jezebel, who calls herself a prophetess, ᶜto teach and seduce My servants to commit sexual immorality and eat things sacrificed to idols. ²¹And I gave her time to ᵃrepent of her sexual immorality, and she did not repent. ²²Indeed I will cast her into a sickbed, and those who commit adultery with her into great tribulation, unless they repent of ᵃtheir deeds. ²³I will kill her children with death, and all the churches shall know that I am He who searchesᵃ the minds and hearts. And I will give to each one of you according to your works.

²⁴"Now to you I say, ᵃand to the rest in Thyatira, as many as do not have this doctrine, who have not known the depths of Satan, as they say, I ᵇwill put on you no other burden. ²⁵But hold fast what you have till I come. ²⁶And he who overcomes, and keeps My works until the end, to him I will give power over the nations—

²⁷ '*He shall rule them with a rod of iron;*
    *They shall be dashed to pieces like the potter's vessels*'—

as I also have received from My Father; ²⁸and I will give him the morning star.

²⁹"He who has an ear, let him hear what the Spirit says to the churches." '

## The Dead Church

**3** "And to the ᵃangel of the church in Sardis write,

'These things says He who has the seven Spirits of God and the seven stars: "I know your works, that you have a name that you are alive, but you are dead. ²Be watchful, and strengthen the things which remain, that are ready to die, for I have not found your works perfect before ᵃGod. ³Remember therefore how you

---

**2:19** ᵃ NU, M *faith, service*  ᵇ *perseverance*  **2:20** ᵃ NU, M *against you that you tolerate*  ᵇ M *your wife Jezebel*  ᶜ NU, M *and teaches and seduces*  **2:21** ᵃ NU, M *repent, and she does not want to repent of her sexual immorality.*  **2:22** ᵃ NU, M *her*  **2:23** ᵃ *examines*  **2:24** ᵃ NU, M omit *and*  ᵇ NU, M omit *will*  **3:1** ᵃ Or *messenger*  **3:2** ᵃ NU, M *My God*

**2:20 Jezebel.** Queen to King Ahab and a model of wickedness in the OT (1 Kin. 16:31–33; 18:4; 21:25–26; 2 Kin. 9:22). **sexual . . . idols.** Used as symbols to represent false worship (see notes on Rev. 2:14–15).

**2:22 tribulation.** Those who compromise and accept false worship to avoid suffering find that suffering comes naturally when one is apart from God.

**2:23 her children.** Those who follow the teachings of false worship by the church leadership; they are her spiritual children.

**2:24 depths of Satan.** Satan tempts people with the promise of greater wisdom if they follow his ways. See Gen. 3:5–6.

**2:27** Contains a clear reference to Ps. 2:9.

**2:28 morning star.** Christ Himself. See 22:16; Dan. 12:3.

**2:29** For the first time in the seven church letters, this phrase comes after the overcomer promise. In the first three letters it comes before the overcomer promise.

**3:1 Sardis.** A city 30 miles (50 km) southeast of Thyatira; an impressive mountaintop acropolis, like Pergamos. Historically, it may represent the sterility of Protestant orthodoxy after the spiritual fervor of the Reformation was past (17th–18th centuries), since the city's name means "that which remains." **seven Spirits . . . seven stars.** God not only sends the message but the means to accept it (see 1:4, 20).

**3:3 come . . . as a thief.** Second Coming language (Matt. 24:42–43; 1 Thess. 5:2; 2 Pet. 3:10) applied to the local situation of a specific church. The church's judgment will come at an unexpected time.

have received and heard; hold fast and repent. Therefore if you will not watch, I will come upon you as a thief, and you will not know what hour I will come upon you. **4** [a]You have a few names [b]even in Sardis who have not defiled their garments; and they shall walk with Me in white, for they are worthy. **5**He who overcomes shall be clothed in white garments, and I will not blot out his name from the Book of Life; but I will confess his name before My Father and before His angels.

**6**"He who has an ear, let him hear what the Spirit says to the churches." '

### The Faithful Church

**7**"And to the [a]angel of the church in Philadelphia write,

'These things says He who is holy, He who is true, *"He who has the key of David, He who opens and no one shuts, and shuts and no one opens"*: **8**"I know your works. See, I have set before you an open door, [a]and no one can shut it; for you have a little strength, have kept My word, and have not denied My name. **9**Indeed I will make *those* of the synagogue of Satan, who say they are Jews and are not, but lie—indeed I will make them come and worship before your feet, and to know that I have loved you. **10**Because you have kept [a]My command to persevere, I also will keep you from the hour of trial which shall come upon the whole world, to test those who dwell on the earth. **11**[a]Behold, I am coming quickly! Hold fast what you have, that no one may take your crown. **12**He who overcomes, I will make him a pillar in the temple of My God, and he shall go out no more. I will write on him the name of My God and the name of the city of My God, the New Jerusalem, which comes down out of heaven from My God. And *I will write on him* My new name.

**13**"He who has an ear, let him hear what the Spirit says to the churches." '

---

**3:4** [a] NU, M *Nevertheless you* [b] NU, M omit *even* **3:7** [a] Or *messenger* **3:8** [a] NU, M *which no one can shut* **3:10** [a] Lit. *the word of My patience* **3:11** [a] NU, M omit *Behold*

**3:4 not defiled their garments.** They were faithful to Christ.

**3:5 white garments.** See v. 18; 6:11; 7:9; 19:8. **not blot out.** See Ex. 32:32–33. Not take away their heavenly citizenship. **the Book of Life.** Lists the names of the saved, like an ancient register of citizens. For more on the books used in the judgment, see 20:15; 21:27; Dan. 7:9–14; Luke 10:20. **confess.** We have a personal advocate in the judgment. See Matt. 10:32.

**3:7 Philadelphia.** Means "brotherly love." A city 25 miles (40 km) southeast of Sardis. In a historical sense, this church's experience may represent the missionary fervor and gospel advancement of 19th-century Christianity, since it was an important stop on the postal route in the empire. **holy . . . true.** The characteristics of God that guided His people in this era (see 6:10; Is. 40:25). **key of David.** Symbolic of the power to control access to the OT kingdom of David (Is. 22:20–22), a position similar to the chief of staff. Jesus, the Son of David, controls access to the kingdom of God and its storehouse of blessings (Matt. 16:19; 2 Cor. 1:20).

**3:8 open door.** The door of salvation through witness or missionary opportunities (see 1 Cor. 16:9; Col. 4:3).

**3:9 synagogue of Satan.** Jewish opponents of the faithful in Philadelphia (see also note on 2:9).

**3:10 keep you.** God's protective care for His people. **hour of trial.** God will not allow us to face more than we can handle (John 16:12; 1 Cor. 10:13).

**3:11 I am coming quickly.** See 1:1; 22:7, 11–12, 20. "Quickly" is a relative term. Certainly with only one church left, the time cannot be long. **Hold fast.** One can lose one's salvation by letting go of Christ. This church is called to persevere in faith and action. **crown.** See note on 2:10.

**3:12 pillar . . . temple.** The weak (v. 8) become strong and vitally useful. **New Jerusalem.** See 21:2; 21:9—22:5. The overcomer will be placed at the governing center of the universe (see 3:21; 7:14–17).

## The Lukewarm Church

**14** "And to the [a]angel of the church [b]of the Laodiceans write,

'These things says the Amen, the Faithful and True Witness, the Beginning of the creation of God: **15** "I know your works, that you are neither cold nor hot. I could wish you were cold or hot. **16** So then, because you are lukewarm, and neither [a]cold nor hot, I will vomit you out of My mouth. **17** Because you say, 'I am rich, have become wealthy, and have need of nothing'—and do not know that you are wretched, miserable, poor, blind, and naked— **18** I counsel you to buy from Me gold refined in the fire, that you may be rich; and white garments, that you may be clothed, *that* the shame of your nakedness may not be revealed; and anoint your eyes with eye salve, that you may see. **19** As many as I love, I rebuke and chasten.[a] Therefore be [b]zealous and repent. **20** Behold, I stand at the door and knock. If anyone hears My voice and opens the door, I will come in to him and dine with him, and he with Me. **21** To him who overcomes I will grant to sit with Me on My throne, as I also overcame and sat down with My Father on His throne.

**22** "He who has an ear, let him hear what the Spirit says to the churches." ' "

---

3:14 [a] Or *messenger* [b] NU, M *in Laodicea*  3:16 [a] NU, M *hot nor cold*  3:19 [a] *discipline* [b] *eager*

**3:14 Laodiceans.** Laodicea was about 45 miles (70 km) southeast of Philadelphia and 90 miles (140 km) east of Ephesus. It was known for its wealth, medical school, and lukewarm water supply and thus may represent the lukewarm condition of the church in today's world. **Amen.** This church is God's "amen" to the world at the end of time. **Witness.** God will use this church as His witness and thus will be with them in the work (see 1:5). **Beginning . . . creation.** Can mean "first in time" ("beginning") or "first in rank" ("ruler"). Either way, the phrase functions as a title of Jesus who is the initiator of creation as the Creator (John 1:1–3) and thus the Ruler of all things (1:17; Col. 1:15–16). The phrase also points to Adam at the beginning as the original ruler of God's creation (Gen. 1:26–28). Jesus, as the second Adam (Rom. 5:12–19; 1 Cor. 15:45), also has that title. For this reason it is not a coincidence that creation is a key topic at the end of time.

**3:15–16 lukewarm.** Hot and cold waters are refreshing and medicinal. Lukewarm water is usually disappointing or even repulsive.

**3:17 need of nothing.** Monetary wealth is often associated with spiritual poverty; the rich do not feel their need. Laodicea's self-deception is the natural human condition (Jer. 17:9).

**3:18 gold.** Represents saving faith (1 Pet. 1:7). **white garments.** Meaning clean from impurity (see note on Rev. 3:5). The option here is white clothes or no clothes. **eye salve.** So Laodicea can see her own lack of authenticity. See note on v. 17.

**3:19** God's love is the source of His discipline (see Heb. 12:5–11).

**3:20 stand . . . knock.** See Song 5:2–6. Laodicea has locked Jesus out. He does not force His way in, but instead invites them to open the door themselves. Elsewhere in the NT, Christ's position at the door or at the gates shows the nearness of His Return (Luke 12:36; compare Matt. 24:33; Mark 13:29; James 5:9).

**3:21** See Phil. 2:6–11 and note on 3:12. This text sets the stage for the next four chapters, which concern God's throne (Rev. 4), the Lamb joining God on His throne (chap. 5), and how the saints overcome and join Jesus on His throne (chaps. 6–7).

## The Throne Room of Heaven
*(Is. 6:1–3)*

**4** After these things I looked, and behold, a door *standing* open in heaven. And the first voice which I heard *was* like a trumpet speaking with me, saying, "Come up here, and I will show you things which must take place after this."

²Immediately I was in the Spirit; and behold, a throne set in heaven, and *One* sat on the throne. ³ᵃAnd He who sat there was like a jasper and a sardius stone in appearance; and *there was* a rainbow around the throne, in appearance like an emerald. ⁴Around the throne *were* twenty-four thrones, and on the thrones I saw twenty-four elders sitting, clothed in white ᵃrobes; and they had crowns of gold on their heads. ⁵And from the throne proceeded lightnings, ᵃthunderings, and voices. Seven lamps of fire *were* burning before the throne, which are the ᵇ seven Spirits of God.

⁶Before the throne *there* ᵃ*was* a sea of glass, like crystal. And in the midst of the throne, and around the throne, *were* four living creatures full of eyes in front and in back. ⁷The first living creature *was* like a lion, the second living creature like a calf, the third living creature had a face like a man, and the fourth living creature *was* like a flying eagle. ⁸*The* four living creatures, each having six wings, were full of eyes around and within. And they do not rest day or night, saying:

> "Holy, ᵃ holy, holy,
> Lord God Almighty,
> Who was and is and is to come!"

⁹Whenever the living creatures give glory and honor and thanks to Him who sits on the throne, who lives forever and ever, ¹⁰the twenty-four elders fall down before Him who sits on the

---

**4:3** ᵃ M omits *And He who sat there was,* making the following a description of the throne.   **4:4** ᵃ NU, M *robes, with crowns*   **4:5** ᵃ NU, M *voices, and thunderings.*   ᵇ M omits *the*   **4:6** ᵃ NU, M add *something like*   **4:8** ᵃ M has *holy* nine times.

**4:1—5:14** Introduction to the seven seals of 6:1—8:1. Each sequence of seven (e.g., churches, seals, trumpets) is introduced with a vision set in the heavenly sanctuary, as is the final vision of the New Jerusalem. The immediate focus moves from earthly things (chaps. 2–3) to the heavenly throne room (see 4:1). The primary focus also moves from the "things which are" to the "things which will take place after this" (1:19; 4:1).

**4:1–11** Chap. 4 does not describe an event within the seven church eras, but rather is a description of the throne room of God. The heavenly throne is the central feature of this chapter; it is the symbol of royal authority. God rules all things and is worthy of worship because He made all things.

**4:1 standing open.** The door is already open when John views it. **Come up here.** In a vision John ascends to heaven. This makes it clear that the scenes of chaps. 1–3 all take place on earth. See note on 1:12.

**4:2 in the Spirit.** See note on 1:10. **throne.** Appears as a central feature in the rest of the book; represents royal power and authority. Note that all three members of the Godhead or Trinity appear in the sanctuary/throne room scenes of chaps. 4–5 (God the Father, 4:2; the Holy Spirit, 4:5; 5:6; Jesus, 5:5–6). See also 1:4–5; 22:16–21.

**4:3 rainbow.** Symbol of God's mercy after the flood (Gen. 9:8–17). See also Rev. 10:1; Ezek. 1:28.

**4:4 twenty-four elders.** Probably representatives of redeemed humanity. See Matt. 27:51–53; Eph. 4:8. **crowns.** See note on Rev. 2:10.

**4:5 lightnings . . . voices.** See also 8:5; 11:19; 16:18. **lamps.** Translates a different word than the one translated "lampstands" in chap. 1, probably indicating that these lamps are not the same as the earlier ones, which were to represent the seven churches. **seven Spirits.** Symbolic reference to the Holy Spirit. See notes on 1:4–5; 5:6.

**4:6 sea of glass.** Also in 15:2. Perhaps similar to what is described in Ex. 24:10, or the laver (water basin) in the OT sanctuary (Ex. 30:17–21; 1 Kin. 7:23–25). **four living creatures.** See Ezek. 1:5–21.

**4:7 flying eagle.** Can be translated either eagle or vulture.

**4:8 six wings . . . Holy, holy, holy.** See Is. 6:2–3. John saw creatures with combined features from Ezek. 1 and Is. 6. **Who was . . . to come.** See note on Rev. 1:4–5.

**4:9 Whenever.** Since "they do not rest day or night" (v. 8), the heavenly throne room is a scene of continued worship (v. 10).

**4:10 cast their crowns.** Recognition that the victory crowns (see note on 2:10) were earned by the only One worthy of worship.

throne and worship Him who lives forever and ever, and cast their crowns before the throne, saying:

<sup>11</sup> "You are worthy, <sup>a</sup>O Lord,
  To receive glory and honor and power;
  For You created all things,
  And by Your will they <sup>b</sup>exist and were created."

## The Lamb Takes the Scroll

**5** And I saw in the right *hand* of Him who sat on the throne a scroll written inside and on the back, sealed with seven seals. <sup>2</sup>Then I saw a strong angel proclaiming with a loud voice, "Who is worthy to open the scroll and to loose its seals?" <sup>3</sup>And no one in heaven or on the earth or under the earth was able to open the scroll, or to look at it.

<sup>4</sup>So I wept much, because no one was found worthy to open <sup>a</sup>and read the scroll, or to look at it. <sup>5</sup>But one of the elders said to me, "Do not weep. Behold, the Lion of the tribe of Judah, the Root of David, has prevailed to open the scroll and <sup>a</sup>to loose its seven seals."

<sup>6</sup>And I looked, <sup>a</sup>and behold, in the midst of the throne and of the four living creatures, and in the midst of the elders, stood a Lamb as though it had been slain, having seven horns and seven eyes, which are the seven Spirits of God sent out into all the earth. <sup>7</sup>Then He came and took the scroll out of the right hand of Him who sat on the throne.

## Worthy Is the Lamb

<sup>8</sup>Now when He had taken the scroll, the four living creatures and the twenty-four elders fell down before the Lamb, each having a harp, and golden bowls full of incense, which are the prayers of the saints. <sup>9</sup>And they sang a new song, saying:

  "You are worthy to take the scroll,
    And to open its seals;

---

**4:11** <sup>a</sup> NU, M *our Lord and God*  <sup>b</sup> NU, M *existed*   **5:4** <sup>a</sup> NU, M omit *and read*   **5:5** <sup>a</sup> NU, M omit *to loose*   **5:6** <sup>a</sup> NU, M *I saw in the midst . . . a Lamb standing*

**4:11** God is worshiped because He is Creator.

**5:1–14** A moment of crisis in the heavenly throne room.

**5:1** *scroll . . . seven seals.* The content of the scroll cannot be read until all seven seals are broken. In chap. 7 it is clear that God's people were the ones being sealed. Thus, possible meanings of the scroll are the Book of Life (13:8; 21:27), the Book of the Covenant (Deut. 17:18–20; 2 Kin. 11:12–17), the title deed to the universe (see Jer. 32:6–15), or the judgment scroll of Ezekiel (Ezek. 2:9—3:3). The codex book form (in general use today) was invented around the time Revelation was written. John clearly has a scroll form in mind here as indicated by the concept of seals and also that in his mind such books can be rolled up (see 6:14).

**5:2** *strong angel.* See 10:1; 18:2, 21. High ranking and authoritative. *worthy.* To be worthy is to have demonstrated fitness for a specific role (Luke 15:19; John 1:27).

**5:3** *heaven . . . earth . . . under the earth.* Expresses the universal scope of the problem.

**5:5** *Lion . . . of Judah.* A Messianic title. See Gen. 49:8–10. **Root of David.** See Is. 11:1, 10. The Messiah comes from the line of David. *prevailed.* Same word as "overcome" in 3:21.

**5:6** *Lamb.* Used 28 times in Revelation to refer to the crucified, risen, and glorified Jesus Christ. *slain.* Sacrificed for sin (Is. 53:7; John 1:29). *seven horns.* The Lamb is the all-powerful ruler in each of the church eras (Dan. 7:8, 20, 24). *seven eyes . . . seven Spirits of God.* The Holy Spirit who bears witness to Christ (John 15:26) in each of the church eras. Jesus was enthroned in heaven on the day of Pentecost (Acts 2). His enthronement triggered the outpouring of the Spirit on earth.

**5:7** By taking the scroll, the Lamb demonstrates that judgment and authority on earth have been assigned to Him.

**5:8** *golden bowls . . . incense.* OT sanctuary images. *prayers.* The actions of the Lamb are in response to the prayers of the saints.

**5:9–10** *new song.* In response to the one-time act of the cross. The sacrifice of Christ on the cross was the decisive moment in the cosmic conflict (the great spiritual battle of salvation history between Christ and Satan; see note on 12:7–9). In 4:11 worship occurs on account of creation. Here it occurs on account of salvation. Both motivations are beautifully symbolized and expressed in the biblical mandate for worshiping God through observing the seventh-day Sabbath (Ex. 20:11; Deut. 5:15).

For You were slain,
And have redeemed us to God by Your blood
Out of every tribe and tongue and people and nation,
10 And have made ᵃus kings ᵇ and priests to our God;
And ᶜwe shall reign on the earth."

¹¹Then I looked, and I heard the voice of many angels around the throne, the living creatures, and the elders; and the number of them was ten thousand times ten thousand, and thousands of thousands, ¹²saying with a loud voice:

"Worthy is the Lamb who was slain
To receive power and riches and wisdom,
And strength and honor and glory and blessing!"

¹³And every creature which is in heaven and on the earth and under the earth and such as are in the sea, and all that are in them, I heard saying:

"Blessing and honor and glory and power
*Be* to Him who sits on the throne,
And to the Lamb, forever and ᵃever!"

¹⁴Then the four living creatures said, "Amen!" And the ᵃtwenty-four elders fell down and worshiped ᵇHim who lives forever and ever.

### First Seal: The Conqueror

**6** Now I saw when the Lamb opened one of the ᵃseals; and I heard one of the four living creatures saying with a voice like thunder, "Come and see." ²And I looked, and behold, a white horse. He who sat on it had a bow; and a crown was given to him, and he went out conquering and to conquer.

---

**5:10** ᵃ NU, M *them*  ᵇ NU *a kingdom*  ᶜ NU, M *they*  **5:13** ᵃ M adds *Amen*  **5:14** ᵃ NU, M omit *twenty-four*  ᵇ NU, M omit *Him who lives forever and ever*  **6:1** ᵃ NU, M *seven seals*

**5:10 *kings and priests.*** See note on 1:5–6.

**5:11 *ten thousand . . . thousands.*** An indefinitely large number. See Dan. 7:10.

**5:12–14** These verses look forward to the glorious conclusion of the cosmic conflict (see note on 5:9–10). The Lamb and the Father receive worship and praise together (see 22:1, 3). In first-century Judaism, "God" was distinguished from all else as the creator and ruler of the universe and the only one worthy of worship. In the New Testament, Jesus possesses all the qualities and prerogatives that belonged only to God in Judaism (see also John 1:3; Rev. 1:5–6; 3:14, 21).

**6:1–17** focus moves from events in heaven to the events on earth that occur as results of the breaking of the seals on the scrolls in each of the seven church eras. They span events from the cross (Rev. 6:1) to the Second Coming (8:1).

**6:1–8** The series of four horses recalls Zech. 1:8–17; 6:1–8. The colors of the horses are related to the character of each rider.

**6:1 *Lamb.*** See notes on 5:6–7. ***one of . . . creatures.*** See notes on 4:6–8. ***voice like thunder.*** Probably the lion-like creature of 4:6–8.

**6:2 *white horse.*** Probably represents the victory of Christ or the gospel, as these symbols are positive in Revelation: "white" (3:4–5; 19:11), "crown" (2:10; 14:14), "conquering" (overcoming; 3:21; 5:5). See Ps. 45:3–5. Unlike the other three, this horse produces no afflictions.

## Second Seal: Conflict on Earth

**3**When He opened the second seal, I heard the second living creature saying, "Come ᵃand see." **4**Another horse, fiery red, went out. And it was granted to the one who sat on it to take peace from the earth, and that *people* should kill one another; and there was given to him a great sword.

## Third Seal: Scarcity on Earth

**5**When He opened the third seal, I heard the third living creature say, "Come and see." So I looked, and behold, a black horse, and he who sat on it had a pair of scalesᵃ in his hand. **6**And I heard a voice in the midst of the four living creatures saying, "A ᵃquart of wheat for a ᵇdenarius, and three quarts of barley for a denarius; and do not harm the oil and the wine."

## Fourth Seal: Widespread Death on Earth

**7**When He opened the fourth seal, I heard the voice of the fourth living creature saying, "Come and see." **8**So I looked, and behold, a pale horse. And the name of him who sat on it was Death, and Hades followed with him. And ᵃpower was given to them over a fourth of the earth, to kill with sword, with hunger, with death, and by the beasts of the earth.

## Fifth Seal: The Cry of the Martyrs

**9**When He opened the fifth seal, I saw under the altar the souls of those who had been slain for the word of God and for the testimony which they held. **10**And they cried with a loud voice, saying, "How long, O Lord, holy and true, until You judge and avenge our blood on those who dwell on the earth?" **11**Then a white robe was given to each of them; and it was said to them that they should rest a little while longer, until both *the number of* their fellow servants and their brethren, who would be killed as they *were,* was completed.

---

**6:3** ᵃ NU, M omit *and see*  **6:5** ᵃ *balances*  **6:6** ᵃ Gr. *choinix*, about 1 quart  ᵇ About 1 day's wage for a worker  **6:8** ᵃ *authority*

**6:4 fiery red.** Represents war and bloodshed. **peace.** Probably the peace of the gospel (1:4). **kill one another.** Civil war. For a gospel-oriented interpretation of civil war, see Matt. 10:34–36; Luke 12:49–51. Rejection of the gospel produces strife, persecution, and confusion.

**6:5 black.** As white was a positive symbol (see note on 6:2), black was an absence of the positive as falsehood crept in. **scales.** A crossbar with scales at either end for determining weights.

**6:6 quart.** Roughly the amount of grain a person eats in a day. With the kind of pricing listed here people would have to work all day just to feed one person. These are famine conditions. From a gospel perspective this is perhaps famine for the word of God (Amos 8:11). Grain, oil, and wine were the three main crops of Canaan (Deut. 7:13; Hos. 2:8, 22). Since grain has more shallow roots than grapevines or olive trees, the expressions in this verse fit the ancient context.

**6:8 pale.** Yellowish-green, the ashen appearance of the dead. **Hades.** The grave (Job 17:13; Song 8:6). Rejection of the gospel results in death. The four horses well represent the initial surge of the gospel followed by the decline and apostasy of the church into the Middle Ages.

**6:9 altar.** Altar of burnt offering (Ex. 27:1–8; 29:12). It was the only altar in the sanctuary with activity at its base (Ex. 29:12; Deut. 12:27). **souls.** In the Hebrew context, the soul (or being; see note on Gen. 2:7) is the whole person. These represent the martyrs of earlier ages (Rev. 6:4) whose shed blood (16:6; John 16:2) cries out to God for justice as did Abel's (Gen. 4:10). This passage does not comment on the state of human beings in death but is a symbolic picture of God's care for the martyrs, His memory of them, and the need for justice and judgment.

**6:10 judge . . . and avenge.** This cry for God's judgment ascends to heaven in 8:3–4; its final fulfillment is in 19:1–2. **those who dwell on the earth.** Description of the wicked in Revelation (3:10; 13:8, 12).

**6:11 white robe.** Symbol of Christ's righteousness (3:4–5; Matt. 22:11–13). **rest.** God's justice comes at the time of His choosing.

## Sixth Seal: Cosmic Disturbances

¹²I looked when He opened the sixth seal, and ᵃbehold, there was a great earthquake; and the sun became black as sackcloth of hair, and the ᵇmoon became like blood. ¹³And the stars of heaven fell to the earth, as a fig tree drops its late figs when it is shaken by a mighty wind. ¹⁴Then the sky ᵃreceded as a scroll when it is rolled up, and every mountain and island was moved out of its place. ¹⁵And the kings of the earth, the great men, ᵃthe rich men, the commanders, the mighty men, every slave and every free man, hid themselves in the caves and in the rocks of the mountains, ¹⁶and said to the mountains and rocks, "Fall on us and hide us from the face of Him who sits on the throne and from the wrath of the Lamb! ¹⁷For the great day of His wrath has come, and who is able to stand?"

## The Sealed of Israel

**7** After these things I saw four angels standing at the four corners of the earth, holding the four winds of the earth, that the wind should not blow on the earth, on the sea, or on any tree. ²Then I saw another angel ascending from the east, having the seal of the living God. And he cried with a loud voice to the four angels to whom it was granted to harm the earth and the sea, ³saying, "Do not harm the earth, the sea, or the trees till we have sealed the servants of our God on their foreheads." ⁴And I heard the number of those who were sealed. One hundred *and* forty-four thousand of all the tribes of the children of Israel *were* sealed:

⁵     of the tribe of Judah twelve thousand *were* sealed;
      of the tribe of Reuben twelve thousand *were* ᵃsealed;
      of the tribe of Gad twelve thousand *were* sealed;
⁶     of the tribe of Asher twelve thousand *were* sealed;
      of the tribe of Naphtali twelve thousand *were* sealed;
      of the tribe of Manasseh twelve thousand *were* sealed;

---

6:12 ᵃ NU, M omit *behold*  ᵇ NU, M *whole moon*   6:14 ᵃ Or *split apart*   6:15 ᵃ NU, M *the commanders, the rich men,*   7:5 ᵃ NU, M omit *sealed* in vv. 5b–8b.

**6:12–14** The language here recalls the day of the Lord passages in the OT (Is. 13:10–13; 34:4; Ezek. 32:7–8; Amos 8:8–10). **great earthquake.** See also Rev. 11:13; 16:18. **sun . . . moon . . . stars.** Similar events are described in Matt. 24:29. Bible scholars associated these harbingers of the end time with specific and remarkable events occurring in the 18th and 19th centuries: the great Lisbon earthquake in 1755, the "Dark Day" in 1780, and the famous "falling of the stars" in 1833. Rev. 6:14 makes clear that even greater catastrophes will occur just before the end.

**6:16 wrath.** God sometimes allows and sometimes enforces the consequences of sin (e.g., the various curses listed in Genesis 3). This is "anger" in a measured, legal sense, not mindless rage.

**6:17 great day of His wrath.** At the Second Coming. See note on 7:1–17.

**7:1–17** There are two sections in the chapter: the 144,000 (vv. 1–8) and the great multitude (vv. 9–17). They are both metaphors for God's end-time people. Both provide the answer to the question of 6:17: "Who is able to stand?"

**7:1 four angels.** May correspond to the four living creatures of 4:6–8. **four winds.** Agents of God's judgment often associated with all the earth (Dan. 7:2; 8:8). See Zech. 6:5. **land . . . sea.** Sources of the two beasts of chap. 13.

**7:2 another angel.** Commander of the four, probably Christ. **seal.** Sign of God's ownership and authority (9:4; 14:1; 2 Tim. 2:19). Possible reference to the Sabbath; see note on Rev. 13:16–17.

**7:3 Do not harm . . . till.** The final judgments on the wicked do not take place until God's people are ready. See Ezek. 9:1–7.

**7:4 I heard the number.** Of God's end-time people. See also 9:16 and context. **One hundred and forty-four thousand.** 12 x 12 x 1000. Probably represents the totality of Israel. A symbol of God's end-time people. The New Jerusalem commemorates the twelve tribes and the twelve apostles (21:12–14).

**7:5–8** The twelve tribes are not listed in birth order. Joseph and Levi replace Dan and Ephraim in the usual list of twelve (Num. 34:13–29; Josh. 13–19).

⁷ of the tribe of Simeon twelve thousand *were* sealed;
of the tribe of Levi twelve thousand *were* sealed;
of the tribe of Issachar twelve thousand *were* sealed;
⁸ of the tribe of Zebulun twelve thousand *were* sealed;
of the tribe of Joseph twelve thousand *were* sealed;
of the tribe of Benjamin twelve thousand *were* sealed.

## A Multitude from the Great Tribulation

⁹After these things I looked, and behold, a great multitude which no one could number, of all nations, tribes, peoples, and tongues, standing before the throne and before the Lamb, clothed with white robes, with palm branches in their hands, ¹⁰and crying out with a loud voice, saying, "Salvation *belongs* to our God who sits on the throne, and to the Lamb!" ¹¹All the angels stood around the throne and the elders and the four living creatures, and fell on their faces before the throne and worshiped God, ¹²saying:

"Amen! Blessing and glory and wisdom,
Thanksgiving and honor and power and might,
*Be* to our God forever and ever.
Amen."

¹³Then one of the elders answered, saying to me, "Who are these arrayed in white robes, and where did they come from?"

¹⁴And I said to him, [a]"Sir, you know."

So he said to me, "These are the ones who come out of the great tribulation, and washed their robes and made them white in the blood of the Lamb. ¹⁵Therefore they are before the throne of God, and serve Him day and night in His temple. And He who sits on the throne will dwell among them. ¹⁶They shall neither hunger anymore nor thirst anymore; the sun shall not strike them, nor any heat; ¹⁷for the Lamb who is in the midst of the throne will shepherd them and lead them to [a]living

---

7:14 [a] NU, M *My lord*   7:17 [a] NU, M *fountains of the waters of life*

**7:9 looked.** John only heard the number of the 144,000, but he sees the great multitude. In Revelation, what John hears and then sees is always a different description of the same person or thing. See 1:10–12; 5:5–6; 17:1, 3; 21:9–10. **great multitude.** Appears again in 19:1–7. **no one could number.** Contrast with 144,000. **all nations . . . tongues.** Contrast with twelve tribes of Israel. **palm branches.** Used for feasts and celebrations (Lev. 23:40; John 12:13).

**7:10–12** A series of acclamations that recall 5:12–13.

**7:13 elders.** See note on 4:4.

**7:14 out of the great tribulation.** See note on 3:10. **washed their robes.** Represents the righteousness of Christ which is received by faith that expresses itself in righteous action (19:7–8).

**7:15–17** A description of the condition and activity of God's redeemed people after the Second Coming of Christ. For more on the New Earth, see 21:1–5.

**7:15 the throne . . . temple.** See 3:21 and 4:2. Saved humanity will serve God in the governing center of the universe—the throne room, which is the temple. **serve.** Translates a word that expresses priestly, sacrificial service. **dwell.** Translates a word usually associated with living in a tent. Used to express His acceptance and protection of them.

**7:16 sun . . . heat.** Scorching heat is characteristic of the plagues in Rev. 16. Their earthly trials are over.

**7:17 Lamb . . . throne.** Reaffirms deity of Christ. Vv. 15–17 use "God" and "Lamb" interchangeably. **tear.** See 21:4.

fountains of waters. And God will wipe away every tear from their eyes."

### Seventh Seal: Prelude to the Seven Trumpets

**8** When He opened the seventh seal, there was silence in heaven for about half an hour. ²And I saw the seven angels who stand before God, and to them were given seven trumpets. ³Then another angel, having a golden censer, came and stood at the altar. He was given much incense, that he should offer *it* with the prayers of all the saints upon the golden altar which was before the throne. ⁴And the smoke of the incense, with the prayers of the saints, ascended before God from the angel's hand. ⁵Then the angel took the censer, filled it with fire from the altar, and threw *it* to the earth. And there were noises, thunderings, lightnings, and an earthquake.

⁶So the seven angels who had the seven trumpets prepared themselves to sound.

### First Trumpet: Vegetation Struck

⁷The first angel sounded: And hail and fire followed, mingled with blood, and they were thrown to the ᵃearth. And a third of the trees were burned up, and all green grass was burned up.

### Second Trumpet: The Seas Struck

⁸Then the second angel sounded: And *something* like a great mountain burning with fire was thrown into the sea, and a third of the sea became blood. ⁹And a third of the living creatures in the sea died, and a third of the ships were destroyed.

### Third Trumpet: The Waters Struck

¹⁰Then the third angel sounded: And a great star fell from heaven, burning like a torch, and it fell on a third of the rivers and on the springs of water. ¹¹The name of the star is Wormwood. A third of the waters became wormwood, and many men died from the water, because it was made bitter.

---

**8:7** ᵃ NU, M add *and a third of the earth was burned up*

**8:1 silence.** Contrast the loud praise of chap. 5. The final act of history is left unsaid, to be presented later.

**8:2–6** Introduces the seven trumpets, which are judgments on the wicked in response to the prayers of the saints in 6:9–10 (see 9:4, 20–21). They span the time from the cross (the beginning of intercession, see notes on 6:1–17; 8:3–4) to the Second Coming (11:15–19). The combined imagery of 8:3–5 is that of intercession followed by judgment.

**8:2 trumpets.** In the OT, trumpets are used in worship, battle, celebrations (Num. 10:1–10), and warning of coming judgment (Lev. 23:23–32). Here they are associated with prayer and introduce judgment.

**8:3–4** Probably based on the daily service in the OT sanctuary, which occurred in the courtyard and Holy Place (Ex. 29:38–42; 30:1–8). The introductory visions in Revelation (1:12–20; chaps. 4–5; 8:2–6) use imagery from the Holy Place up until 11:19, where the focus shifts to the Most Holy Place. See note on 11:19. **censer.** A fire pan for burning incense. **altar.** Golden incense altar of the OT sanctuary (9:13; Ex. 30:1–8). **incense.** Probably represents the righteousness of Christ, which makes the prayers of the saints acceptable to God.

**8:5** The response to the prayers of the saints is judgment on the wicked. See Ezek. 10:2.

**8:7 hail . . . earth.** Recalls Ex. 9:22–26 and Ezek. 38:22–23. **a third.** Indicates judgment that is not full and final. See also Rev. 8:8–12; 9:15, 18. May represent the judgments on Jerusalem in the first century (see Luke 21:20–24; 23:28–31).

**8:8–9 something like.** Indicates the language is not to be taken literally here. **great mountain . . . fire.** Volcanic imagery. See Jer. 51:24–25, 63–64. **blood.** Allusion to Ex. 7:17–21. May represent the fall of Rome in the fifth century A.D.

**8:10–11 star fell.** See note on 9:1. See also Is. 14:12–15. **rivers . . . springs.** Images of spiritual nourishment (Ps. 1:3; John 7:37–39). **Wormwood.** Bitter-tasting plant; a metaphor for idolatry (Deut. 29:17–18). From a historical perspective this may represent the apostasy of the church in the Middle Ages.

### Fourth Trumpet: The Heavens Struck

¹²Then the fourth angel sounded: And a third of the sun was struck, a third of the moon, and a third of the stars, so that a third of them were darkened. A third of the day ᵃdid not shine, and likewise the night.

¹³And I looked, and I heard an ᵃangel flying through the midst of heaven, saying with a loud voice, "Woe, woe, woe to the inhabitants of the earth, because of the remaining blasts of the trumpet of the three angels who are about to sound!"

### Fifth Trumpet: The Locusts from the Bottomless Pit

**9** Then the fifth angel sounded: And I saw a star fallen from heaven to the earth. To him was given the key to the ᵃbottomless pit. ²And he opened the bottomless pit, and smoke arose out of the pit like the smoke of a great furnace. So the sun and the air were darkened because of the smoke of the pit. ³Then out of the smoke locusts came upon the earth. And to them was given power, as the scorpions of the earth have power. ⁴They were commanded not to harm the grass of the earth, or any green thing, or any tree, but only those men who do not have the seal of God on their foreheads. ⁵And ᵃthey were not given *authority* to kill them, but to torment them *for* five months. Their torment *was* like the torment of a scorpion when it strikes a man. ⁶In those days men will seek death and will not find it; they will desire to die, and death will flee from them.

⁷ The shape of the locusts was like horses prepared for battle. On their heads were crowns of something like gold, and their faces *were* like the faces of men. ⁸They had hair like women's hair, and their teeth were like lions' *teeth*. ⁹And they had breastplates like breastplates of iron, and the sound of their wings *was* like the sound of chariots with many horses running into battle. ¹⁰They had tails like scorpions, and there were stings in their tails. Their power *was* to hurt men five months. ¹¹And they had as king over

---

8:12 ᵃ *had no light*   8:13 ᵃ NU, M *eagle*   9:1 ᵃ Lit. *shaft of the abyss*   9:5 ᵃ The locusts

**8:12** Recalls Ex. 10:21–23. The intensity of the light is reduced. **sun . . . moon . . . stars.** Images of God's blessing (Ps. 84:11; Is. 30:26). May represent the deepening apostasy of the Middle Ages or the skepticism of the Renaissance and the Enlightenment.

**8:13 Woe.** Disaster or judgment. The three woes correspond to the fifth through seventh trumpets (9:12; 11:14).

**9:1–11** The fifth trumpet uses the imagery of a demonic attack to demonstrate Satan's tormenting power in the lives of the wicked (vv. 5–6), but also his helplessness against the faithful people of God (v. 4). This section may represent the reality and spiritual consequences of the secularism and skepticism that have become increasingly dominant over the years. It has also been interpreted as the political and military impact of militant Islam on apostate Christendom.

**9:1 star fallen.** Refers back to the star of the third trumpet (8:10). The events of the fifth trumpet are a consequence of the third. **was given.** Divine passive. God is in full control of this plague; see also 9:3, 5. **bottomless pit.** Where the demons are confined (Luke 8:31), but also the place from which the beasts come (Rev. 11:7; 17:8).

**9:2 smoke . . . furnace.** Recalls Sodom and Sinai (Gen. 19:28; Ex. 19:18).

**9:3 scorpions.** Demonic imagery; see Luke 10:17–20.

**9:4 seal of God.** See note on 7:2. Demons cannot harm God's faithful people. See also Rom. 8:35–39. Normal locusts harm vegetation; these "locusts" attack people.

**9:5–6 five months.** May represent the lifespan of locusts, the duration of the flood (Gen. 7:24; 8:3), or 150 years (see note on year-day principle in Rev. 11:2). **In those days . . . not find it.** This plague results in psychological, rather than physical, torment.

**9:7–10** Horrific collection of images that recalls Joel 2:1–11. Heightens the horror of this plague.

**9:10 tails.** Instruments of torture. Represent lying prophets in Is. 9:15. Satan uses false beliefs to torment people. **five months.** See note on 9:5–6.

**9:11 angel.** Probably Satan. The actions of Satan and demons are subject to God's limits and control. Literal locusts have no leader (Prov. 30:27), so these locusts are figurative. **Abaddon . . . Apollyon.** Hebrew and Greek names that mean "destroyer." It is Satan rather than God who is the destroyer. It is Satan who causes sickness, harm and, psychological anguish, not God.

them the angel of the bottomless pit, whose name in Hebrew *is* ᵃAbaddon, but in Greek he has the name ᵇApollyon.

¹²One woe is past. Behold, still two more woes are coming after these things.

### Sixth Trumpet: The Angels from the Euphrates

¹³Then the sixth angel sounded: And I heard a voice from the four horns of the golden altar which is before God, ¹⁴saying to the sixth angel who had the trumpet, "Release the four angels who are bound at the great river Euphrates." ¹⁵So the four angels, who had been prepared for the hour and day and month and year, were released to kill a third of mankind. ¹⁶Now the number of the army of the horsemen *was* two hundred million; I heard the number of them. ¹⁷And thus I saw the horses in the vision: those who sat on them had breastplates of fiery red, hyacinth blue, and sulfur yellow; and the heads of the horses *were* like the heads of lions; and out of their mouths came fire, smoke, and brimstone. ¹⁸By these three *plagues* a third of mankind was killed—by the fire and the smoke and the brimstone which came out of their mouths. ¹⁹For ᵃtheir power is in their mouth and in their tails; for their tails *are* like serpents, having heads; and with them they do harm.

²⁰But the rest of mankind, who were not killed by these plagues, did not repent of the works of their hands, that they should not worship demons, and idols of gold, silver, brass, stone, and wood, which can neither see nor hear nor walk. ²¹And they did not repent of their murders or their ᵃsorceries or their sexual immorality or their thefts.

### The Mighty Angel with the Little Book

**10** I saw still another mighty angel coming down from heaven, clothed with a cloud. And a rainbow *was* on his head, his face *was* like the sun, and his feet like pillars of fire. ²He had a little book open in his hand. And he set his right foot on

---

9:11 ᵃ Lit. *Destruction*   ᵇ Lit. *Destroyer*   9:19 ᵃ NU, M *the power of the horses*   9:21 ᵃ NU, M *drugs*

**9:13–21** The sixth trumpet describes religious opposition toward God and His people. The humanistic philosophies of Marxism and evolution (see note on 9:17–19) sprang up during the same time as the events in chaps. 10 and 11. The sixth trumpet has also been interpreted in relation to historical events in the Middle East.

**9:13** *voice.* Probably Christ's. *golden altar.* See note on 8:3–4. Intercession is still going on; see also 10:11 and 11:13.

**9:14** *four angels.* Recalls 7:1–3. *Euphrates.* See 16:12. The northeastern boundary of the promised land (Gen. 15:18). Beyond it lay ancient Babylon and Assyria (Is. 8:5–8).

**9:15** *the hour . . . year.* Has been interpreted as a span of 391 years (based on 12 months of 30 days). See notes on 11:2 and Dan. 7:25. Another view is that the expression refers to a specific point in time.

**9:16** *two hundred million.* This is the demonic counterpart (200,000,000) of God's army (144,000). *I heard.* See 7:4.

**9:17–19** Parallels description of vv. 7–9. *their mouths . . . tails.* Adds a new weapon (mouth, symbolizing new philosophies) to the power of the previous plague (v. 10).

**9:20–21** The language of these verses recalls OT Babylon (Is. 47:9–12; Dan. 5:23–24). *murders . . . thefts.* Recalls the sixth, seventh, and ninth commandments (Ex. 20:13–16).

**10:1—11:14** Part of the sixth trumpet (see note on 8:13). This section provides a view of God's people toward the end of history still during the sixth church era.

**10:1** *another mighty angel.* See 5:2. This scene also parallels the picture of Christ in 1:13–16. *cloud.* See 1:7; 14:14; Matt. 17:5; 24:30. *rainbow.* See note on Rev. 4:3. *pillars of fire.* See Ex. 13:21–22; 14:24.

**10:2** *little book . . . open.* Contrast 5:1–4; Dan. 12:4. The scroll is already open when the vision begins. It should be noted that after the little book is opened, the book of Daniel is featured in Revelation in a way that it was not prior to chap. 10. See, for example, the relationships between Dan. 7:7 and Rev. 12:3; 13:1; Dan. 7:14, 27 and Rev. 11:15; Dan. 7:3–6 and Rev. 13:1–2; Dan. 7:13–14 and Rev. 14:14. Consider the issue of worship in Dan. 3 and Rev. 13:4, 8, 12, 15; 14:7, 9, 11, and the connection between the sealed parts of Daniel (8:26; 9:24; 12:4, 9) and Revelation (10:4; 22:10). Compare Dan. 12:7; 7:25 with Rev. 11:2–3; 12:6, 14; 12:17; 14:12, 7 regarding the persecution of God's people over time (e.g., 42 months, 1,260 days). Also compare Dan. 8:11–14, 26 with Rev. 11:1, 19; 13:6 (a focus on the sanctuary/temple).

the sea and *his* left *foot* on the land, ³and cried with a loud voice, as *when* a lion roars. When he cried out, seven thunders uttered their voices. ⁴Now when the seven thunders ᵃuttered their voices, I was about to write; but I heard a voice from heaven saying ᵇto me, "Seal up the things which the seven thunders uttered, and do not write them."

⁵The angel whom I saw standing on the sea and on the land raised up his ᵃhand to heaven ⁶and swore by Him who lives forever and ever, who created heaven and the things that are in it, the earth and the things that are in it, and the sea and the things that are in it, that there should be delay no longer, ⁷but in the days of the sounding of the seventh angel, when he is about to sound, the mystery of God would be finished, as He declared to His servants the prophets.

### John Eats the Little Book

⁸Then the voice which I heard from heaven spoke to me again and said, "Go, take the little book which is open in the hand of the angel who stands on the sea and on the earth."

⁹So I went to the angel and said to him, "Give me the little book."

And he said to me, "Take and eat it; and it will make your stomach bitter, but it will be as sweet as honey in your mouth."

¹⁰Then I took the little book out of the angel's hand and ate it, and it was as sweet as honey in my mouth. But when I had eaten it, my stomach became bitter. ¹¹And ᵃhe said to me,

---

10:4 ᵃ NU, M *sounded,*   ᵇ NU, M omit *to me*   10:5 ᵃ NU, M *right hand*   10:11 ᵃ NU, M *they*

**10:3 lion.** See 5:5. **seven thunders.** Revelation gives no clue as to their meaning. But see Ps. 29:3–9.

**10:4 voice from heaven.** Not the mighty angel of 10:1–2; either God or Christ. This same unidentified voice reappears in 10:8; 11:2; 14:2, 13; and 18:4.

**10:5–6 raised up . . . and ever.** Strong allusion to Dan. 12:4–7. Dan. 12 is the climax of a section that begins with a vision (Dan. 8:3–14) followed by a series of explanations of that vision (Dan. 8:15–26; 9:24–27; 11:1—12:3; 12:4–13). So in alluding to Rev. 12:4–7, John is inviting the reader to consider all of Dan. 8–12 as background to Rev. 10. **delay no longer.** Literally "time will be no more." This is not the end of history, but the point in history where the time prophecies of Dan. 8–12 (8:13–14; 12:7–12) come to an end. Using the historicist method of interpretation, many scholars identify the end of two of Daniel's major prophecies (the 1,260-day and the 2,300-day; see note on Dan. 12:4) in the years A.D. 1798 and 1844. The period that follows is "the time of the end" (Dan. 11:40; 12:4, 9). See note on 11:2 concerning the year-day principle.

**10:7 but.** Despite the declaration of v. 6, "there should be delay no longer," time continues. **mystery of God.** Revealed through the gospel (see Rom. 16:25–27; Eph. 3:3–7). **finished.** Meaning to fulfill or complete. Understanding of God's requirements and salvation is accomplished just before the seventh trumpet of warning sounds. **declared.** Translates the verb form of "gospel." The "time of the end" includes the final proclamation of the gospel (see Rev. 14:6–7). That final proclamation of the gospel ends with the close of probation when the seventh trumpet stops sounding.

**10:8–10 book.** Understood to be the prophecies of Daniel (see Dan. 12:4), because the book of Daniel has now become a strong emphasis in Revelation (see note on 10:2). **bitter . . . honey.** John's experience eating the book of Daniel was similar to that of Ezekiel (see Ezek. 2:8—3:3), and prophetically anticipates the time when Daniel's prophecies came to an end in the mid-19th century. At that time, many looked for the Second Coming of Christ and were disappointed. See note on 10:5–6.

**10:11 prophesy again about.** The last word could also be translated "to," as it is in 14:6. In fact, the similar wording of 14:6 ("nation, tribe, tongue, and people") indicates that the content of that passage is the message that needs to be given here also. John's experience and responsibility become representative of God's end-time remnant. Those who experienced the bitterness of disappointment in regard to Daniel's time prophecies must continue to preach and prophesy, as is expressed also in 14:6–13. See note on 14:6–13.

"You must prophesy again about many peoples, nations, tongues, and kings."

### The Two Witnesses

**11** Then I was given a reed like a measuring rod. ᵃAnd the angel stood, saying, "Rise and measure the temple of God, the altar, and those who worship there. ²But leave out the court which is outside the temple, and do not measure it, for it has been given to the Gentiles. And they will tread the holy city underfoot *for* forty-two months. ³And I will give *power* to my two witnesses, and they will prophesy one thousand two hundred and sixty days, clothed in sackcloth."

⁴These are the two olive trees and the two lampstands standing before the ᵃGod of the earth. ⁵And if anyone wants to harm them, fire proceeds from their mouth and devours their enemies. And if anyone wants to harm them, he must be killed in this manner. ⁶These have power to shut heaven, so that no rain falls in the days of their prophecy; and they have power over waters to turn them to blood, and to strike the earth with all plagues, as often as they desire.

### The Witnesses Killed

⁷When they finish their testimony, the beast that ascends out of the bottomless pit will make war against them, overcome them, and kill them. ⁸And their dead bodies *will lie* in the street of the great city which spiritually is called Sodom and Egypt, where also ᵃour Lord was crucified. ⁹Then *those* from the peoples, tribes, tongues, and nations ᵃwill see their dead

---

11:1 ᵃ NU, M omit *And the angel stood*   11:4 ᵃ NU, M *Lord*   11:8 ᵃ NU, M *their*   11:9 ᵃ NU, M *see . . . and will not allow*

**11:1–14** Part of the sixth trumpet; see note on 8:13. Explains the "prophesy again" of 10:11.

**11:1 reed.** Bamboo-like cane. See 21:15 and Ezek. 40:3–5. In Ezekiel the temple was measured in order to restore it (Ezek. 43:7–9). **the temple of God.** In the NT temple language can be applied to the literal temple in Jerusalem (Matt. 21:12; John 2:20), Jesus Himself (Matt. 12:6; John 2:21), the sanctuary in heaven (Heb. 9:11), the church (1 Cor. 3:16–17; Eph. 2:21), and the human body (1 Cor. 6:19). The most likely meaning here is the heavenly sanctuary. Prophesying again (10:11) in the time of the end will include a message about the heavenly sanctuary. **measure.** The measuring is a work of judgment, separating the faithful from the unfaithful. **altar.** The burnt-offering altar in the court outside the OT sanctuary. **those who worship there.** The people of God, the remnant, who must "prophesy again" (Rev. 10:11).

**11:2 leave out.** Same word as "cast . . . out" in John 9:34–35. **tread.** See Rev. 14:20; 19:15; Luke 21:24. **the holy city.** See Rev. 21:2. Here represents the faithful people of God, in contrast to the wicked great city (11:8). **forty-two months.** See also 13:5. Same as 1,260 days (11:3; 12:6) or 3 1/2 years (12:14; Dan. 7:25 and 12:7). In the Bible, days and years are often treated as equivalent (Lev. 25:1–7; Num. 14:34; Ezek. 4:4–6). Historicist interpreters, therefore, have generally understood the period of 1,260 prophetic days to mean 1,260 literal years running from A.D. 538 to 1798. See also note on Dan. 7:25.

**11:3–14** Has been applied to the French Revolution (as an enemy of Scripture) and the final proclamation of the gospel.

**11:3 two witnesses.** Based on Moses and Elijah (see vv. 5–6). They could represent Scripture (the Law and the Prophets) or God's people (Acts 1:8). **one thousand . . . days.** See notes on Rev. 11:2 and Dan. 7:25. **sackcloth.** Signifies mourning (Gen. 37:34; Is. 22:12) for they are neglected.

**11:4 two olive . . . lampstands.** See Zech. 4:2–3. Trees (Rev. 9:4) and lampstands (1:20) represent God's people in Revelation.

**11:5–6** These verses are strongly based on the actions of Moses and Elijah. **fire . . . enemies.** 2 Kin. 1:10–12. **shut heaven.** 1 Kin. 17:1. **blood.** Ex. 7:17–21.

**11:7–8 finish.** See 10:7. **bottomless pit.** See note on 9:1. **kill them.** The same fate as their Lord in 11:8. **in the street.** Denial of burial shows great disrespect (Ps. 79:2–23; Jer. 8:1–2). **the great city.** Usually Babylon in Revelation (14:8; 18:1–4). Babylon is a symbol of the end time, religious opposition to God. **where . . . crucified.** Physically just outside of Jerusalem, but spiritually inside Babylon. The same spiritual kingdom was at work in the French Revolution as at Jesus's crucifixion.

bodies three-and-a-half days, and not allow their dead bodies to be put into graves. ¹⁰And those who dwell on the earth will rejoice over them, make merry, and send gifts to one another, because these two prophets tormented those who dwell on the earth.

### The Witnesses Resurrected

¹¹Now after the three-and-a-half days the breath of life from God entered them, and they stood on their feet, and great fear fell on those who saw them. ¹²And ᵃthey heard a loud voice from heaven saying to them, "Come up here." And they ascended to heaven in a cloud, and their enemies saw them. ¹³In the same hour there was a great earthquake, and a tenth of the city fell. In the earthquake seven thousand people were killed, and the rest were afraid and gave glory to the God of heaven.

¹⁴The second woe is past. Behold, the third woe is coming quickly.

### Seventh Trumpet: The Kingdom Proclaimed

¹⁵Then the seventh angel sounded: And there were loud voices in heaven, saying, "The ᵃkingdoms of this world have become *the kingdoms* of our Lord and of His Christ, and He shall reign forever and ever!" ¹⁶And the twenty-four elders who sat before God on their thrones fell on their faces and worshiped God, ¹⁷saying:

> "We give You thanks, O Lord God Almighty,
>   The One who is and who was ᵃand who is to come,
>   Because You have taken Your great power and reigned.
> ¹⁸ The nations were angry, and Your ᵃwrath has come,
>   And the time of the dead, that they should be judged,
>   And that You should reward Your servants the prophets and
>     the saints,

---

11:12 ᵃ M *I*   11:15 ᵃ NU, M *kingdom . . . has become the kingdom*   11:17 ᵃ NU, M omit *and who is to come*   11:18 ᵃ *anger*

**11:10 send . . . another.** See Est. 9:22. **prophets.** The two witnesses fulfill the "again prophesy" of 10:11. See also 11:3, 6. **those who . . . earth.** See note on 6:10.

**11:11 breath of life.** Gen. 2:7; Ezek. 37:5–10. Reading the two witnesses as Scripture, this scene portrays the great revival of interest in the Bible after the French Revolution. Reading them as the church, this scene elaborates on the final proclamation of the gospel introduced in 10:7, 11.

**11:12 ascended . . . cloud.** This reminds the reader of Christ's ascension, as recorded in Acts 1:8–11.

**11:13 great earthquake.** See 6:12. **the rest.** Could be translated "remnant." See 12:17. **afraid . . . glory.** The response called for in 14:7. If 11:14 represents the close of human probation (see note on 10:7), this is the final, positive response to the end-time preaching of the gospel (10:11; 14:6–7).

**11:14 woe.** See note on 8:13.

**11:15 kingdom.** In the preaching of Jesus the "kingdom" was both present and future. That same tension occurs in the use of "kingdom" here and in 12:10.

**11:16 twenty-four elders.** See note on 4:4.

**11:18** While the end of the seventh trumpet's blast signals the close of human probation (see note on 10:7), there are still events (chap. 15–16) that must take place before the Second Coming. **nations . . . angry.** See 12:17. **Your wrath.** The seven bowl plagues (see 15:1). **dead . . . judged.** The execution of the judgment of the dead is detailed in 20:11–15. **reward.** 22:11–12. **destroy . . . earth.** See 19:1–2. The language of this verse anticipates the major turning points of the second half of the book (chaps. 12–22).

And those who fear Your name, small and great,
And should destroy those who destroy the earth."

¹⁹Then the temple of God was opened in heaven, and the ark of ᵃHis covenant was seen in His temple. And there were lightnings, noises, thunderings, an earthquake, and great hail.

### The Woman, the Child, and the Dragon

**12** Now a great sign appeared in heaven: a woman clothed with the sun, with the moon under her feet, and on her head a garland of twelve stars. ²Then being with child, she cried out in labor and in pain to give birth.

³And another sign appeared in heaven: behold, a great, fiery red dragon having seven heads and ten horns, and seven diadems on his heads. ⁴His tail drew a third of the stars of heaven and threw them to the earth. And the dragon stood before the woman who was ready to give birth, to devour her Child as soon as it was born. ⁵She bore a male Child who was to rule all nations with a rod of iron. And her Child was caught up to God and His throne. ⁶Then the woman fled into the wilderness, where she has a place prepared by God, that they should feed her there one thousand two hundred and sixty days.

### Satan Thrown Out of Heaven

⁷And war broke out in heaven: Michael and his angels fought with the dragon; and the dragon and his angels fought, ⁸but they ᵃdid not prevail, nor was a place found for ᵇthem in heaven any longer. ⁹So the great dragon was cast out, that serpent of old,

---

**11:19** ᵃ M *the covenant of the Lord*   **12:8** ᵃ *were not strong enough*   ᵇ M *him*

**11:19** The reference is to the heavenly sanctuary, which introduces chaps. 12–14. Up to this point in Revelation, all the sanctuary introductions have alluded to the Holy Place of the sanctuary (see note on 8:3–4). This one, as indicated by the presence of the ark, moves into the Most Holy Place. For more on the sanctuary, see Ex. 25:8–9; Dan. 8:14. **the ark.** God's "throne" in the OT sanctuary (Ex. 25:10–22). Contained the Ten Commandments (Ex. 20:1–17), which are featured in Rev. 12:17; 14:12. **lightnings . . . hail.** See note on 4:5.

**12:1–17** An overview of history from the birth of Christ to the final events. Includes allusions to the original conflict in heaven (vv. 4, 7–9).

**12:1 sign.** The vision to follow is largely symbolic. **woman.** Represents the people of God (Song 6:10; Is. 54:5–6), both before (Rev. 12:5) and after (v. 6) the earthly ministry of Jesus.

**12:2 in pain . . . birth.** See Gen. 3:16; Mic. 4:8–10.

**12:3 dragon.** Represents Satan (v. 9; Gen. 3:15). Also represents the civil power of Rome (Rev. 12:5; Matt. 2:3–18). **heads . . . horns.** Allusion to the total number of heads and horns in Dan. 7:3–7. **diadems.** Royal crowns.

**12:4 third . . . stars.** Stars probably represent angels here as is the case in 1:20. Satan encouraged the rebellion of one-third of the angels in heaven before creation (13:8).

**12:5 male Child.** Reference to the birth of Christ. See also Ps. 2:7–9. **caught up.** Ascension of Christ (Acts 1:8–11).

**12:6** Parallels v. 14. **woman.** Describes the ongoing experience of the church (see notes on 12:1). **wilderness.** Place of protection (Hos. 2:14). **one thousand . . . days.** See notes on Rev. 11:2 and Dan. 7:25.

**12:7–9 war . . . in heaven.** Immediate context is the ascension of Christ and His enthronement in heaven (vv. 5, 10). But allusions to Is. 14:12–19 and Gen. 3:1–15 indicate a flashback to the original war in heaven. The heavenly war is not about guns and tanks. It is a war of words, having to do with Satan's accusations against God and His people (12:10) and their testimony against him on the basis of the cross (12:11). For more on the origin of sin, see Ezek. 28:12–19. **Michael.** Christ. **serpent.** Recalls Gen. 3:1–15. **cast out.** Satan's influence focused on earth as a result of the war and Adam's fall; he and his angels were excluded from all influence in heaven on account of the cross and the ascension (Rev. 12:10–12; compare John 12:31).

called the Devil and Satan, who deceives the whole world; he was cast to the earth, and his angels were cast out with him.

¹⁰Then I heard a loud voice saying in heaven, "Now salvation, and strength, and the kingdom of our God, and the power of His Christ have come, for the accuser of our brethren, who accused them before our God day and night, has been cast down. ¹¹And they overcame him by the blood of the Lamb and by the word of their testimony, and they did not love their lives to the death. ¹²Therefore rejoice, O heavens, and you who dwell in them! Woe to the inhabitants of the earth and the sea! For the devil has come down to you, having great wrath, because he knows that he has a short time."

### The Woman Persecuted

¹³Now when the dragon saw that he had been cast to the earth, he persecuted the woman who gave birth to the male *Child*. ¹⁴But the woman was given two wings of a great eagle, that she might fly into the wilderness to her place, where she is nourished for a time and times and half a time, from the presence of the serpent. ¹⁵So the serpent spewed water out of his mouth like a flood after the woman, that he might cause her to be carried away by the flood. ¹⁶But the earth helped the woman, and the earth opened its mouth and swallowed up the flood which the dragon had spewed out of his mouth. ¹⁷And the dragon was enraged with the woman, and he went to make war with the rest of her offspring, who keep the commandments of God and have the testimony of Jesus [a]Christ.

---

**12:17** [a] NU, M omit *Christ*

**12:10 kingdom . . . Christ.** The enthronement of Christ took place at the ascension (3:21; 5:1–14). **accuser . . . cast down.** Though expelled from heaven at the beginning, Satan's accusations retained influence in heaven until the cross (Job 1:9–11). His accusations are now proven false (Rom. 8:35–39; Col. 2:15).

**12:11 overcame him.** This verse offers a "how to" of overcoming (see 2:7). **blood . . . death.** Believers overcome through faith in Christ's death and resurrection, which frees them from the fear of death, enabling them to present a fearless testimony.

**12:12 Woe.** The earth now has Satan's undivided attention. **short time.** While evil and suffering may seem endless, their doom is sure.

**12:13** The scene returns to earth (v. 6).

**12:14 two wings . . . nourished.** Allusions to the exodus (Ex. 19:4). **time . . . time.** Strong allusion to Dan. 7:25 and 12:7. See notes on Rev. 11:2, 12:6, and Dan. 7:25.

**12:15–16 serpent spewed.** Allusion to the overwhelming flood of population in which there are deceptive words of the serpent in Gen. 3:1–6. **earth helped.** Toward the end of the 1,260 years (see note on Rev. 11:2), many forces combined to bring an end to the religious persecution of the Middle Ages: the Reformation, the Enlightenment, and the American Revolution.

**12:17 dragon . . . offspring.** The two sides in the final conflict on earth. **war.** Not only will **the commandments** be important at the end of time, but there will be a conflict over them. This verse sets the stage for the next two chapters, which feature the agents and activities of the dragon in chap. 13 and the identity and message of the last-day woman (the church) in chap. 14. **the rest of her offspring.** Often translated as "remnant," one of several designations for the end-time people of God in Revelation. Two chief characteristics of the end-time remnant: obedience to **the commandments of God** and possession of **the testimony of Jesus Christ** (see Rev. 19:10)—a visionary gift like John's (see note on 1:2). In addition, the context suggests that the remnant appear in history after the 1,260 days/years (12:14; see note on 11:2).

## The Beast from the Sea

**13** Then ᵃI stood on the sand of the sea. And I saw a beast rising up out of the sea, having ᵇseven heads and ten horns, and on his horns ten crowns, and on his heads a blasphemous name. ²Now the beast which I saw was like a leopard, his feet were like *the feet of* a bear, and his mouth like the mouth of a lion. The dragon gave him his power, his throne, and great authority. ³And I saw one of his heads as if it had been mortally wounded, and his deadly wound was healed. And all the world marveled and followed the beast. ⁴So they worshiped the dragon who gave authority to the beast; and they worshiped the beast, saying, "Who *is* like the beast? Who is able to make war with him?"

⁵And he was given a mouth speaking great things and blasphemies, and he was given authority to ᵃcontinue for forty-two months. ⁶Then he opened his mouth in blasphemy against God, to blaspheme His name, His tabernacle, and those who dwell in heaven. ⁷It was granted to him to make war with the saints and to overcome them. And authority was given him over every ᵃtribe, tongue, and nation. ⁸All who dwell on the earth will worship him, whose names have not been written in the Book of Life of the Lamb slain from the foundation of the world.

⁹If anyone has an ear, let him hear. ¹⁰He who leads into captivity shall go into captivity; he who kills with the sword must be killed with the sword. Here is the ᵃpatience and the faith of the saints.

---

13:1 ᵃ NU *he*   ᵇ NU, M *ten horns and seven heads*   13:5 ᵃ M *make war*   13:7 ᵃ NU, M add *and people*
13:10 ᵃ *perseverance*

**13:1–18** This chapter elaborates on chap. 12, particularly the end-time war of the last verse (12:17). In this chapter the dragon gathers two allies for the final conflict. The beast from the sea (an apparent parody of Christ) and the beast from the earth (an apparent parody of the Holy Spirit) suggest a false trinity (16:13–14) in collusion to deceive the world (13:13–14) regarding worship.

**13:1–7** This section describes the history of the sea beast before its end-time activity. It arises **out of the sea** (meaning more densely populated area of the planet; see note on 17:15–16) within history after the lion, bear, leopard, and terrible beast of Dan. 7, speaking with the same blaspheming mouth over the same amount of time as the little horn (Dan. 7:8, 25; 8:10–12) and usurping the work of Christ. Protestant scholars through the centuries have identified this sea beast with the papacy. (Compare descriptions with Dan. 7:3–7, 25; 8:11–14.)

**13:1 horns . . . heads.** See note on 12:3. **crowns.** The crowns have shifted from the heads to the horns (see Rev. 12:3; Dan. 7:4–8). **blasphemous name.** A religious power in opposition to God and His people. See Dan. 7:8, 25.

**13:2 the beast . . . lion.** A composite of Daniel's four beasts (Dan. 7:4–8).

**13:3 mortally wounded.** Literally "slaughtered to death," the same word is translated "slain" in v. 8. The language here recalls the death and resurrection of Christ. Historicist interpreters have long seen the wound to the sea beast as the decline of Rome that culminated in 1798 with the French capture of the Pope. **healed.** Recovers, miraculously, from a fatal wound. Seen by many as the profoundly increasing influence of the papacy on world affairs in the late twentieth and early twenty-first centuries. **marveled.** Fascination that leads to following.

**13:4 Who . . . beast?** The deliberate contrast to Christ is striking, for the name Michael (Christ; 12:7) means "Who is like God?"

**13:5–7** Clear allusions to Daniel (Dan. 7:8, 20–21, 25; 8:9–12). **was given . . . was granted.** Greek passive tense used only for God. While the beast is acting with hostility toward God and His people, God is in ultimate control of events. See also Rev. 17:17. **forty-two months.** See notes on Rev. 11:2 and Dan. 7:25. **tabernacle.** The heavenly sanctuary. Whatever this beast's boasts of power, God monitors and controls earth's history from the vantage point of the heavenly sanctuary/throne room (Rev. 4–5). **authority . . . nation.** The same entities that are here controlled by the beast are the object of the final gospel proclamation (14:6).

**13:8–10** Verbs switch to present and future tenses. The healed and revived beast is central to the final events.

**13:8 Book of Life.** See note on 3:5. **foundation of the world.** The pain of the cross has been in the heart of God from the beginning. See notes on 12:4.

## The Beast from the Earth

**11**Then I saw another beast coming up out of the earth, and he had two horns like a lamb and spoke like a dragon. **12**And he exercises all the authority of the first beast in his presence, and causes the earth and those who dwell in it to worship the first beast, whose deadly wound was healed. **13**He performs great signs, so that he even makes fire come down from heaven on the earth in the sight of men. **14**And he deceives ªthose who dwell on the earth by those signs which he was granted to do in the sight of the beast, telling those who dwell on the earth to make an image to the beast who was wounded by the sword and lived. **15**He was granted *power* to give breath to the image of the beast, that the image of the beast should both speak and cause as many as would not worship the image of the beast to be killed. **16**He causes all, both small and great, rich and poor, free and slave, to receive a mark on their right hand or on their foreheads, **17**and that no one may buy or sell except one who has ªthe mark or the name of the beast, or the number of his name.

**18**Here is wisdom. Let him who has understanding calculate the number of the beast, for it is the number of a man: His number *is* 666.

---

13:14 ª M *my own people*   13:17 ª NU, M *the mark, the name*

**13:11 out of the earth.** Out of a less populated area of the planet (compare with note on 13:1–7). This verse describes the shorter history of the earth beast before its end-time activity. The initial positive symbolic language (**two horns like a lamb**) and strong connections with 12:16 ("the earth," where God's people "the woman" fled from Europe to avoid religious persecution) have suggested to many historicist interpreters that the description of this beast is a reference to the United States of America, which came to power toward the end of the 1,260 years (see note on 11:2), as a Protestant nation with its religious influence. "Lamb" in Revelation refers to Christ, which means this power is Christian. **like a dragon.** It looks Christian but speaks the words of Satan.

**13:12–18** These are the actions of the earth beast and its allies in the final battle.

**13:12 he exercises . . . first beast.** The sea beast is reactivated for final events, but the earth beast, an apparent third player in a false end-time trinity, takes a leading and visible role in its behalf. See also 16:13–14. **deadly wound.** See note on Rev. 13:3.

**13:13** See Matt. 24:24; 2 Thess. 2:8–10. **signs.** This earthly power performs persuasive miracles that establish its authority. See note on John 2:11. **fire . . . from heaven.** Perhaps an intentional similarity to the role of the Holy Spirit in the tongues of fire at Pentecost (Acts 2); as impressive and convincing as Elijah's fire on Mount Carmel (1 Kin. 18).

**13:14–15 those . . . earth.** The wicked (see note on 6:10). **breath.** Could also be translated as "spirit." Allusion to Gen. 2:7. Rev. 13:15–17 represents the climax of the war of 12:17. **image of the beast.** A new character in the drama. It functions at the end as a persecutor and an object of worship, the way the sea beast did earlier. This is a strong allusion to the image-worship in Dan. 3.

**13:16–17 mark.** The replacement for the seal of God, which the Sabbath command represented (Ex. 20:8–11). At the heart of ancient covenants was a seal containing the name, title, and basis for authority of the covenant maker. The Sabbath command plays that role in the Ten Commandments. See note on Rev. 11:19. This allusion to the Sabbath commandment is part of a series of allusions to the first four of the Ten Commandments. The unholy trinity (dragon, sea beast, and earth beast) seeks worship (13:4, 8, 12), sets up an image (13:15), blasphemes God (13:1, 5–6) and replaces the Sabbath command (see note on 14:7) by instituting first-day worship in place of seventh-day (thus seeking to change times and laws; Dan. 7:25). **hand . . . foreheads.** Represents actions and belief respectively. Some accept the mark simply to avoid death (v. 15) and maintain normalcy (v. 17), while others embrace it out of a belief. **name.** See note on 14:1.

**13:18 666.** God's number in Revelation is seven, so a large number that repeatedly emphasizes the number six may represent falling short (see notes on vv. 1–17). Note the emphasis on sixes in Nebuchadnezzar's image of gold in Dan. 3:1. The actual number is written out in the Greek text as the single number "six hundred sixty six."

## The Lamb and the 144,000

**14** Then I looked, and behold, <sup>a</sup>a Lamb standing on Mount Zion, and with Him one hundred *and* forty-four thousand, <sup>b</sup>having His Father's name written on their foreheads. ²And I heard a voice from heaven, like the voice of many waters, and like the voice of loud thunder. And I heard the sound of harpists playing their harps. ³They sang as it were a new song before the throne, before the four living creatures, and the elders; and no one could learn that song except the hundred *and* forty-four thousand who were redeemed from the earth. ⁴These are the ones who were not defiled with women, for they are virgins. These are the ones who follow the Lamb wherever He goes. These were <sup>a</sup>redeemed from *among* men, *being* firstfruits to God and to the Lamb. ⁵And in their mouth was found no <sup>a</sup>deceit, for they are without fault <sup>b</sup>before the throne of God.

## The Proclamations of Three Angels

⁶Then I saw another angel flying in the midst of heaven, having the everlasting gospel to preach to those who dwell on the earth—to every nation, tribe, tongue, and people— ⁷saying with a loud voice, "Fear God and give glory to Him, for the hour of His judgment has come; and worship Him who made heaven and earth, the sea and springs of water."

---

**14:1** <sup>a</sup> NU, M *the*  <sup>b</sup> NU, M add *His name and*   **14:4** <sup>a</sup> M adds *by Jesus*   **14:5** <sup>a</sup> NU, M *falsehood*  <sup>b</sup> NU, M omit the rest of v. 5.

**14:1–20** The previous chapter focuses on the dragon's side in the war for the heart and mind (12:17). Chap. 14 focuses on the remnant's side of the final conflict.

**14:1 Mount Zion.** Synonym for Jerusalem; an allusion to Joel 2:32. Here New Jerusalem. **one hundred . . . thousand.** Based on Joel 2:32, this group is the same as those in Rev. 12:17. See also note on 7:4. **name.** In the Hebrew context, name represents character. To have the name or seal of God (see 7:1–3) on the forehead (contrast 13:17) means to reflect God's character in one's life.

**14:2 thunder.** The first living creature had a voice like thunder (6:1).

**14:3 new song.** See note on 5:9–10. New songs arise from new experiences. **throne . . . elders.** See notes on 4:1–4. **no one . . . song.** It requires the experience of salvation. Those who have experienced salvation from sin will have a unique witness to the character of God throughout eternity. **redeemed from the earth.** To a heavenly location, either literally after the Second Coming or spiritually during the final crisis of 12:17 (see Eph. 2:6).

**14:4 virgins.** Symbol of spiritual purity and loyalty (2 Cor. 11:2). They are ready for the wedding of the Lamb (Rev. 19:7–8). **firstfruits.** They are the first portion of a larger crop (see 14:14–20).

**14:5 no deceit.** Lying is excluded from the New Jerusalem (21:27; 22:15). Contrast 13:13–14; 16:14. **without fault.** First, the 144,000 are accepted in Christ. Second, in following Jesus they have become like Him (see 19:8).

**14:6–13** These three angels actually represent the three last messages to be preached to the earth by the end-time remnant before the Son of Man arrives in the clouds (14:14). These are the messages that were commissioned in 10:11. For more on the mission of the remnant, see 18:1–4.

**14:6 gospel.** Fulfills Matt. 24:14. The first of three angels who proclaim God's final message to the world. In the context of Revelation, the gospel includes the good news of Christ's Second Coming, in which He rescues His people. It also includes the good news about the character of God in contrast with the character of Satan (see notes on 12:7–11).

**14:7 Fear God.** Means "revere, respect, hold in awe" (Ps. 111:10; Prov. 3:7; 9:10). But it can also mean "be afraid" for those who do not hold Him in awe/respect (Rev. 6:15–17). **give glory.** Also connected with the fear of God in 11:13 and 15:4. Giving glory to God includes actions as well as words. See 1 Cor. 6:19; 10:31. **hour . . . has come.** The final judgment begins before the Second Coming. It is the context for the final proclamation of the gospel. **worship . . . sea.** This language makes an unmistakable allusion to the Sabbath command with reference to Creation (Ex. 20:8–11), thus indicating that the Sabbath has particular relevance in end-time gospel proclamation. To rest from one's works is the ideal response to the gospel (see Heb. 4:1–11). The admonitions to "fear" and to "worship" in this verse are placed directly in the larger immediate context of keeping God's commandments (see Rev. 12:17; 14:12), with obvious references to the Decalogue. **springs of water.** The only part of this clause not drawn from Exod. 20:8–11. Likely recalls the flood story (Gen 7:11; 8:2).

⁸And another angel followed, saying, "Babylon*ᵃ* is fallen, is fallen, that great city, because she has made all nations drink of the wine of the wrath of her fornication."

⁹Then a third angel followed them, saying with a loud voice, "If anyone worships the beast and his image, and receives *his* mark on his forehead or on his hand, ¹⁰he himself shall also drink of the wine of the wrath of God, which is poured out full strength into the cup of His indignation. He shall be tormented with fire and brimstone in the presence of the holy angels and in the presence of the Lamb. ¹¹And the smoke of their torment ascends forever and ever; and they have no rest day or night, who worship the beast and his image, and whoever receives the mark of his name."

¹²Here is the ᵃpatience of the saints; here ᵇ *are* those who keep the commandments of God and the faith of Jesus.

¹³Then I heard a voice from heaven saying ᵃto me, "Write: 'Blessed *are* the dead who die in the Lord from now on.' "

"Yes," says the Spirit, "that they may rest from their labors, and their works follow them."

## Reaping the Earth's Harvest

¹⁴Then I looked, and behold, a white cloud, and on the cloud sat *One* like the Son of Man, having on His head a golden crown, and in His hand a sharp sickle. ¹⁵And another angel came out of the temple, crying with a loud voice to Him who sat on the cloud,

---

**14:8** ᵃ NU *Babylon the great is fallen, is fallen, which has made;* M *Babylon the great is fallen. She has made*  **14:12** ᵃ *steadfastness, perseverance*  ᵇ NU, M omit *here are those*   **14:13** ᵃ NU, M omit *to me*

**14:8 Babylon . . . great.** The first mention of Babylon, the focus of God's judgments in Rev. 16–18. See note on 11:7–8. This is a condemnation of corporate, religious opposition to God. The gospel and the judgment are closely related in Scripture (see John 3:18–21). **all nations.** End-time Babylon precipitates worldwide opposition to God. This is elaborated in chap. 17. Babylon in the OT also represented the oppressor of God's people and "confusion" (see Gen. 11:1–9).

**14:9–11 If anyone.** The focus shifts from collective (14:7–8) to individual responsibility in the final crisis. See note on v. 8. **worships . . . hand.** Recalls 13:12–18. **wrath of God.** The seven bowl plagues of chap. 16 (see 11:18; 15:1). **cup . . . indignation.** Allusion to Is. 51:17–23. **brimstone.** Sulphur. See also Rev. 19:20; Gen. 19:24. **forever.** An obvious allusion to Is. 34:8–10. In the Hebrew context, forever is not necessarily absolute; it is long enough to accomplish God's purpose. For more on hell and the punishment of the wicked, see Rev. 20:10; Matt. 10:28.

**14:12 patience.** Means endurance in the context of suffering (13:9–10). Might also imply patiently waiting for Christ's return. **keep the commandments of God.** Obedience to God's law is an essential characteristic of God's people in the end time. **faith of Jesus.** Can mean "faith in Jesus" or "Jesus's faith," meaning what Jesus believed—the doctrines held and taught by Jesus. Recent scholarship has focused on Jesus's "faithfulness." It is Jesus's faithfulness in obedience to and revelation of the Father's character that lies at the core of our salvation. V. 12 has a contextual relation to 12:17 and the conflict pictured in chap. 13.

**14:13 Blessed.** See note on 1:3. **from now on.** Those who die in this context (14:6–12) will not have to experience the trials of the final events. These deaths may include the outcome of the persecution of 13:15. **their works follow them.** Their salvation is secure. See 1 Tim. 5:24–25.

**14:14 cloud . . . Son of Man.** The movements of the Son of Man are often portrayed in the context of clouds, as in His coming to judge (Dan. 7:13–14), His ascension (Acts 1), and His Second Coming (Matt. 24:30). **crown.** See note on Rev. 2:10.

**14:15 temple.** Throne room of God (11:19). **harvest.** Second Coming (Joel 3:12–17).

"Thrust in Your sickle and reap, for the time has come ᵃfor You to reap, for the harvest of the earth is ripe." **¹⁶**So He who sat on the cloud thrust in His sickle on the earth, and the earth was reaped.

### Reaping the Grapes of Wrath

**¹⁷**Then another angel came out of the temple which is in heaven, he also having a sharp sickle.

**¹⁸**And another angel came out from the altar, who had power over fire, and he cried with a loud cry to him who had the sharp sickle, saying, "Thrust in your sharp sickle and gather the clusters of the vine of the earth, for her grapes are fully ripe." **¹⁹**So the angel thrust his sickle into the earth and gathered the vine of the earth, and threw *it* into the great winepress of the wrath of God. **²⁰**And the winepress was trampled outside the city, and blood came out of the winepress, up to the horses' bridles, for one thousand six hundred ᵃfurlongs.

### Prelude to the Bowl Judgments

**15** Then I saw another sign in heaven, great and marvelous: seven angels having the seven last plagues, for in them the wrath of God is complete.

**²**And I saw *something* like a sea of glass mingled with fire, and those who have the victory over the beast, over his image and ᵃover his mark *and* over the number of his name, standing on the sea of glass, having harps of God. **³**They sing the song of Moses, the servant of God, and the song of the Lamb, saying:

> "Great and marvelous *are* Your works,
> Lord God Almighty!
> Just and true *are* Your ways,
> O King of the ᵃsaints!
> **4** Who shall not fear You, O Lord, and glorify Your name?
> For *You* alone *are* holy.

---

14:15 ᵃ NU, M omit *for You*   14:20 ᵃ Lit. *stadia*, about 184 miles in all   15:2 ᵃ NU, M omit *over his mark*   15:3 ᵃ NU, M *nations*

**14:18 angel . . . fire.** Probably the angel of 8:3–5.

**14:19 winepress.** Usually carved out of rock. An upper trough is for pressing grapes with a channel to a lower trough for collecting juice. **wrath of God.** Anticipates the seven bowl plagues of 15:1—16:21.

**14:20 outside the city.** The city is Jerusalem. See Joel 3:12–17. **one thousand six hundred furlongs.** Approximate length of Palestine from north to south. This is a multiple of the number four, which represents worldwide events (Rev. 7:1–3; 14:6).

**15:1–8** Climax of chaps. 12–14 and introduction to the seven bowl plagues.

**15:1 seven last plagues.** See 16:1–21. **complete.** See 11:18. Up to now God has always mitigated judgment with mercy.

**15:2 sea . . . fire.** See note on 4:6.

**15:3 song of Moses.** Recalls Ex. 15:1–18. The judgments of the end are compared with the events of the exodus. **Just . . . ways.** God's actions at the end are acknowledged to be in full harmony with His law and character. This is the bottom line of the cosmic conflict (see note on 5:9–10).

**15:4 fear . . . glorify . . . worship . . . judgments.** Recalls the key words of 14:7. The last gospel message has received a positive response from many.

For all nations shall come and worship before You,
For Your judgments have been manifested."

⁵After these things I looked, and ᵃbehold, the ᵇtemple of the tabernacle of the testimony in heaven was opened. ⁶And out of the ᵃtemple came the seven angels having the seven plagues, clothed in pure bright linen, and having their chests girded with golden bands. ⁷Then one of the four living creatures gave to the seven angels seven golden bowls full of the wrath of God who lives forever and ever. ⁸The temple was filled with smoke from the glory of God and from His power, and no one was able to enter the temple till the seven plagues of the seven angels were completed.

# 16

Then I heard a loud voice from the temple saying to the seven angels, "Go and pour out the ᵃbowls of the wrath of God on the earth."

## First Bowl: Loathsome Sores

²So the first went and poured out his bowl upon the earth, and a ᵃfoul and loathsome sore came upon the men who had the mark of the beast and those who worshiped his image.

## Second Bowl: The Sea Turns to Blood

³Then the second angel poured out his bowl on the sea, and it became blood as of a dead *man;* and every living creature in the sea died.

## Third Bowl: The Waters Turn to Blood

⁴Then the third angel poured out his bowl on the rivers and springs of water, and they became blood. ⁵And I heard the angel of the waters saying:

"You are righteous, ᵃO Lord,
  The One who is and who ᵇwas and who is to be,
  Because You have judged these things.

---

15:5 ᵃ NU, M omit *behold*  ᵇ *sanctuary,* the inner shrine   15:6 ᵃ *sanctuary,* the inner shrine   16:1 ᵃ NU, M *seven bowls*   16:2 ᵃ *severe and malignant,* lit. *bad and evil*   16:5 ᵃ NU, M omit *O Lord*  ᵇ NU, M *was, the Holy One*

**15:5 After . . . looked.** Major break. Vv. 5–8 are a sanctuary introduction to the seven plagues of chap. 16. **temple . . . testimony.** A combined reference to Solomon's temple (1 Kin. 6–8) and the Mosaic tabernacle (Ex. 25–40). "The testimony" refers to the Ten Commandments given to Moses and placed in the tabernacle (Ex. 31:18; 32:15; 34:29). This reference to the Ten Commandments, combined with the reference to the ark (which contained the Ten Commandments) in 11:19, brackets the central section of Revelation (chaps. 12–14) with its emphasis on the first four Commandments (see note on 13:16–17) and particularly the Sabbath (see note on 14:7).

**15:6 out of the temple.** The plagues are the consequence of violating the governing principles of the universe. **pure bright linen.** In most cases violence is repugnant, but in this case it is required by pure, spotless justice.

**15:7 four living creatures.** See notes on 4:6–8. **wrath of God.** See 15:1.

**15:8 no one . . . completed.** See Ex. 40:34–35; 1 Kin. 8:10–11. An empty temple indicates the end of heavenly intercession, signaling the close of human probation on earth.

**16:1–21** The seven trumpets of chaps. 8–11 were the warning messages to the wicked through the seven church eras and, as a result, find some parallels in the bowls, which are the plagues at the end of time. Read literally, the plagues express major ecological disasters that result from God removing His protective hand from the earth.

**16:1 pour out.** Connects this scene with 15:5–8. Events in heaven affect events on earth. The setting of chap. 16 is a series of events beyond the close of probation.

**16:2 sore.** The same word is translated "boils" in Ex. 9:9–11 and indicates leprosy in Lev. 13:18–27. This is probably literal and may represent a global disease outbreak (pandemic). **came upon . . . image.** Recipients of the plagues are the oppressors of Rev. 13:14–17.

**16:4 blood.** Instead of bitterness; compare 8:10–11.

**16:5–7** The punishment here is appropriate to the crime and recalls the question of 6:10. It also contains many echoes of 15:3–4. **angel of the waters.** Same as the angel of third bowl. **who is . . . to be.** See 1:4, 8; 4:8; 11:17.

⁶ For they have shed the blood of saints and prophets,
And You have given them blood to drink.
ᵃFor it is their just due."

⁷And I heard ᵃanother from the altar saying, "Even so, Lord God Almighty, true and righteous *are* Your judgments."

### Fourth Bowl: Men Are Scorched

⁸Then the fourth angel poured out his bowl on the sun, and power was given to him to scorch men with fire. ⁹And men were scorched with great heat, and they blasphemed the name of God who has power over these plagues; and they did not repent and give Him glory.

### Fifth Bowl: Darkness and Pain

¹⁰Then the fifth angel poured out his bowl on the throne of the beast, and his kingdom became full of darkness; and they gnawed their tongues because of the pain. ¹¹They blasphemed the God of heaven because of their pains and their sores, and did not repent of their deeds.

### Sixth Bowl: Euphrates Dried Up

¹²Then the sixth angel poured out his bowl on the great river Euphrates, and its water was dried up, so that the way of the kings from the east might be prepared. ¹³And I saw three unclean spirits like frogs *coming* out of the mouth of the dragon, out of the mouth of the beast, and out of the mouth of the false prophet. ¹⁴For they are spirits of demons, performing signs, *which* go out

---

16:6 ᵃ NU, M omit *For*   16:7 ᵃ NU, M omit *another from*

**16:8–9 scorch men.** In contrast with the fourth trumpet (8:12), here the sun's intensity is increased. **blasphemed . . . God . . . did not repent.** Reverse of 11:13, where judgments led to repentance. Nothing God does changes the hearts of the wicked anymore. The close of probation is grounded less in a divine decree than in the reality of human choice. **give Him glory.** See 11:13; 14:7; 15:4.

**16:10–11 throne.** Seat of authority, normally associated with God in Revelation. See chaps. 4–5 and note on 4:2. **beast.** See 13:2. **darkness.** This is a direct challenge to the beast's authority. The plagues are undermining the beast's control of the earth (13:12).

**16:12 Euphrates.** See note on 9:14. The river was part of Babylon's defense system (Jer. 50:35–38; 51:36–37). Here it represents the political powers of the world (Rev. 17:1, 15). **dried up.** See Is. 44:24–28. Indicates Babylon's loss of political support (Rev. 17:16). **east.** Literally, "sunrise." See Matt. 24:27; Luke 1:78. This verse as a whole recalls the original fall of Babylon to Cyrus and his royal allies. Cyrus came from the east, dried up the River Euphrates, conquered Babylon, delivered God's people, and rebuilt Jerusalem. This root story is echoed throughout Rev. 16–22. See Isa. 45:1–4 and earlier references to Isa. 44 and Jer. 50–51.

**16:13–15** The symbolism in these verses implies the possibility of human decision, so these verses describe events prior to the plagues, the close of probation, and the conclusion of Armageddon.

**16:13 unclean spirits.** See 18:2. Agents of the dragon, beast, and false prophet. **frogs.** Recalls Ex. 8:1–9. **dragon . . . beast . . . false prophet.** The false trinity (dragon, sea beast, and land beast) of Rev. 12–13. Together they make up end-time Babylon (16:19). They meet their end in 19:20; 20:10.

**16:14 demons.** Satanic angels and counterparts to the three angels of 14:6–12. A final, worldwide deception intent on turning people away from the true gospel. **signs.** See 13:13–14. **kings of the earth.** Equivalent to the Euphrates River of 16:12, as defined in 17:15. The "kings of the east" (16:12) are the divine counterpart to these wicked kings.

to the kings ᵃ of the earth and of the whole world, to gather them to the battle of that great day of God Almighty.

¹⁵"Behold, I am coming as a thief. Blessed *is* he who watches, and keeps his garments, lest he walk naked and they see his shame."

¹⁶And they gathered them together to the place called in Hebrew, ᵃ Armageddon.

### Seventh Bowl: The Earth Utterly Shaken

¹⁷Then the seventh angel poured out his bowl into the air, and a loud voice came out of the temple of heaven, from the throne, saying, "It is done!" ¹⁸And there were noises and thunderings and lightnings; and there was a great earthquake, such a mighty and great earthquake as had not occurred since men were on the earth. ¹⁹Now the great city was divided into three parts, and the cities of the nations fell. And great Babylon was remembered before God, to give her the cup of the wine of the fierceness of His wrath. ²⁰Then every island fled away, and the mountains were not found. ²¹And great hail from heaven fell upon men, *each hailstone* about the weight of a talent. Men blasphemed God because of the plague of the hail, since that plague was exceedingly great.

### The Scarlet Woman and the Scarlet Beast

**17** Then one of the seven angels who had the seven bowls came and talked with me, saying ᵃ to me, "Come, I will show you the judgment of the great harlot who sits on many waters, ²with whom the kings of the earth committed fornication, and the inhabitants of the earth were made drunk with the wine of her fornication."

³So he carried me away in the Spirit into the wilderness. And I saw a woman sitting on a scarlet beast *which was* full of names of blasphemy, having seven heads and ten horns. ⁴The woman was arrayed in purple and scarlet, and adorned with gold and

---

16:14 ᵃ NU, M omit *of the earth and*   16:16 ᵃ Lit. *Mount Megiddo;* M *Megiddo*   17:1 ᵃ NU, M omit *to me*

**16:15 thief.** Recalls Matt. 24:43–44; Luke 12:38–40; 1 Thess. 5:1–6. **Blessed.** See note on Rev. 1:3. **garments . . . naked . . . shame.** Allusion to 3:17–18.

**16:16 they.** Translation of singular "he" to point back to the three frogs of v. 14. But the singular may instead refer to Jesus, the one who speaks in v. 15. **Armageddon.** A Hebrew/Greek mixture probably meaning "mountain of Megiddo." Could recall Mount Carmel (1 Kin. 18) or OT battles at Megiddo (Judg. 5:19) in the Valley of Jezreel. Here the intention is not to identify a specific geographical location but to indicate a decisive battle between good and evil. The entire world is called to decide whether to worship the true God or the deception.

**16:17 out of the temple . . . throne.** See 15:6. There is no distinction in Revelation between the heavenly temple and God's throne room.

**16:18 noises . . . earthquake.** See 4:5; 8:5; 11:19.

**16:19 great city.** See note on 11:7–8. **three parts.** See 16:13. **Babylon.** Summary fulfillment of 14:8–11. This verse anticipates the fuller outline of Babylon's fall in chaps. 17–18.

**16:21 blasphemed.** Confirms unwillingness of the wicked to repent during the plagues.

**17:1–18** This chapter elaborates on the sixth and seventh plagues (16:12–21). The primary metaphor is Babylon as a prostitute.

**17:1 one of . . . bowls.** Probably the sixth bowl angel (16:12), as the waters of this verse are associated with Babylon and the waters of Babylon are the Euphrates River. **many waters.** A description of the river of Babylon (Euphrates). See v. 15; Jer. 51:13.

**17:2** See 14:8.

**17:3–6** A vision of the prostitute Babylon riding on a beast.

**17:3 in the Spirit.** See note on 1:10. **wilderness.** See 12:6, 14. The parallels between the two women in the wilderness underscore the Christian origin of the final enemy of God. **woman.** Same as the prostitute of 17:1, 5. **scarlet beast.** See 12:3 and 13:1–2. Represents worldwide political power in support of end-time Babylon. John hears that the prostitute is sitting on many waters (17:1) but sees a woman on a beast instead. See note on 7:9. So the beast and the Euphrates River are symbols of the same thing: political, economic, and military power in support of false religion.

**17:4–5** There are many parallels between the prostitute Babylon and the OT high priest (Ex. 28:1–43). This is a deceptive end-time religious system (see Rev. 16:13, 19), the heir of the medieval union of church and state. **forehead a name.** In Hebrew thought, a reflection of character.

precious stones and pearls, having in her hand a golden cup full of abominations and the filthiness of ᵃher fornication. ⁵And on her forehead a name *was* written:

> MYSTERY, BABYLON THE GREAT,
> THE MOTHER OF HARLOTS AND OF
> THE ABOMINATIONS OF THE EARTH.

⁶I saw the woman, drunk with the blood of the saints and with the blood of the martyrs of Jesus. And when I saw her, I marveled with great amazement.

### The Meaning of the Woman and the Beast

⁷But the angel said to me, "Why did you marvel? I will tell you the ᵃmystery of the woman and of the beast that carries her, which has the seven heads and the ten horns. ⁸The beast that you saw was, and is not, and will ascend out of the bottomless pit and go to ᵃperdition. And those who dwell on the earth will marvel, whose names are not written in the Book of Life from the foundation of the world, when they see the beast that was, and is not, and ᵇyet is.

⁹"Here *is* the mind which has wisdom: The seven heads are seven mountains on which the woman sits. ¹⁰There are also seven kings. Five have fallen, one is, *and* the other has not yet come. And when he comes, he must continue a short time. ¹¹The beast that was, and is not, is himself also the eighth, and is of the seven, and is going to ᵃperdition.

¹²"The ten horns which you saw are ten kings who have received no kingdom as yet, but they receive authority for one hour as kings with the beast. ¹³These are of one mind, and they will give their power and authority to the beast. ¹⁴These will make war with the Lamb, and the Lamb will overcome them, for He is Lord of lords and King of kings; and those *who are* with Him *are* called, chosen, and faithful."

---

17:4 ᵃ M *the fornication of the earth*   17:7 ᵃ *hidden truth*   17:8 ᵃ *destruction*   ᵇ NU, M *shall be present*   17:11 ᵃ *destruction*

**17:6 *of the martyrs of Jesus.*** "Martyr" can also be translated "witness," which sometimes was manifested in the ultimate sacrifice (see 6:9–11). The medieval church produced many martyrs, and end-time Babylon will do the same.

**17:7–18** Explanation of the vision of vv. 3–6.

**17:7 *angel.*** The angel of v. 1 now explains the vision of vv. 3–6. ***carries her.*** She is in a position of control (until v. 16).

**17:8 *ascend . . . pit.*** See 11:7. ***perdition.*** The eternal destruction of the wicked. See 20:10, 14–15. ***the Book of Life.*** See note on 3:5. ***was, and is not.*** A parody of God (1:4; 4:8).

**17:10 *one is.*** The seven heads are consecutive. Since John is the point of reference, the "one is" would be the Rome of his day (v. 18). The five fallen kings would then be Egypt, Assyria, Babylon, Medo-Persia, and Greece. The seventh head would arrive in history sometime between John's day and the end of the world.

**17:11 *eighth.*** The eighth head, the beast of the final crisis. ***of the seven.*** The summation and climax of the prior seven, it functions as an oppressive power.

**17:12 *ten horns.*** See vv. 3–11; 12:3; 13:2; Dan. 7:7–8. They represent a major subgroup of the world's nations, something like NATO. When the ten horns decide to support the beast, a true worldwide political alliance is formed. But it only lasts a short time. ***kingdom as yet.*** These powers did not exist in John's day. ***with the beast.*** At the time of the eighth head (Rev. 17:11), the final crisis.

**17:14 *Lord . . . kings.*** See 19:16–21. ***called . . . faithful.*** The saints, who are sub-kings with the Lamb (1:6; 5:10).

¹⁵Then he said to me, "The waters which you saw, where the harlot sits, are peoples, multitudes, nations, and tongues. ¹⁶And the ten horns which you ᵃsaw on the beast, these will hate the harlot, make her desolate and naked, eat her flesh and burn her with fire. ¹⁷For God has put it into their hearts to fulfill His purpose, to be of one mind, and to give their kingdom to the beast, until the words of God are fulfilled. ¹⁸And the woman whom you saw is that great city which reigns over the kings of the earth."

## The Fall of Babylon the Great

**18** After these things I saw another angel coming down from heaven, having great authority, and the earth was illuminated with his glory. ²And he cried ᵃmightily with a loud voice, saying, "Babylon the great is fallen, is fallen, and has become a dwelling place of demons, a prison for every foul spirit, and a cage for every unclean and hated bird! ³For all the nations have drunk of the wine of the wrath of her fornication, the kings of the earth have committed fornication with her, and the merchants of the earth have become rich through the ᵃabundance of her luxury."

⁴And I heard another voice from heaven saying, "Come out of her, my people, lest you share in her sins, and lest you receive of her plagues. ⁵For her sins ᵃhave reached to heaven, and God has remembered her iniquities. ⁶Render to her just as she rendered ᵃto you, and repay her double according to her works; in the cup which she has mixed, mix double for her. ⁷In the measure that she glorified herself and lived ᵃluxuriously, in the same measure give her torment and sorrow; for she says in her heart, 'I sit *as* queen, and am no widow, and will not see sorrow.' ⁸Therefore her plagues will come in one day—death and mourning and famine. And she will be utterly burned with fire, for strong *is* the Lord God who ᵃjudges her.

---

**17:16** ᵃ NU, M *saw, and the beast*   **18:2** ᵃ NU, M omit *mightily*   **18:3** ᵃ Lit. *strengths*   **18:5** ᵃ NU, M *have been heaped up*   **18:6** ᵃ NU, M omit *to you*   **18:7** ᵃ *sensually*   **18:8** ᵃ NU, M *has judged*

**17:15–16 waters . . . sits.** See note on v. 1. **ten horns.** See note on v. 12. **hate . . . fire.** This event is parallel to the drying up of the River Euphrates in 16:12. **burn her.** See Lev. 21:9. A further confirmation that the prostitute is a religious power.

**17:17** God is ultimately in control of the events of history, including satanic actions (9:1–5; 2 Thess. 2:11). See note on 13:5–7.

**17:18 great city.** See note on 11:7–8. **is . . . reigns.** Continuous present tenses. The great city lies behind all opposition to God throughout history. Babylon represents Satan's kingdom. End-time Babylon will be a deceptive religious replacement for gospel faith. See notes on 13:1–7, 18; 14:8; 17:4–5.

**18:1–24** The fall of Babylon theme continues from chap. 17. There the key image is the execution of a prostitute (17:1, 4–5, 16). Here the metaphor is the sacking of a wealthy city (18:9–19).

**18:1 another angel.** Different from the one in 17:1. **illuminated.** Foretaste of the New Earth (21:23; 22:5).

**18:2–3 Babylon . . . fallen.** Not yet the physical fall, but a declaration of her spiritual condition. **dwelling place . . . prison.** This demonic character is startling in an organization that proclaims itself to be on God's side (see note on 17:18). **drunk.** See 14:8; 17:2.

**18:4 my people.** God distinguishes between an organization that opposes Him and individuals in that organization who are faithful to God. This is the final call of the gospel to join God's remnant people. For more on the remnant, see 12:17; 14:6–12.

**18:5 For.** Could be translated "because." Vv. 5–7 list the actions that have provoked Babylon's legal sentence.

**18:6 Render . . . to you.** The punishment fits the crime. **repay her double.** An ancient metaphor for full and final punishment (Jer. 17:18).

**18:7 glorified . . . luxuriously.** Her glory and luxury came at the expense of others, so it becomes a basis of her legal sentence. Corporate selfishness is expressed in exploitation of others in order to gain wealth and power for the institution. See note on 18:11.

**18:8 plagues.** The plagues of chap. 16 are still future at this point. This is a legal sentence that precedes in time the carrying out of that sentence. **fire.** See 17:16.

## The World Mourns Babylon's Fall

⁹"The kings of the earth who committed fornication and lived luxuriously with her will weep and lament for her, when they see the smoke of her burning, ¹⁰standing at a distance for fear of her torment, saying, 'Alas, alas, that great city Babylon, that mighty city! For in one hour your judgment has come.'

¹¹"And the merchants of the earth will weep and mourn over her, for no one buys their merchandise anymore: ¹²merchandise of gold and silver, precious stones and pearls, fine linen and purple, silk and scarlet, every kind of citron wood, every kind of object of ivory, every kind of object of most precious wood, bronze, iron, and marble; ¹³and cinnamon and incense, fragrant oil and frankincense, wine and oil, fine flour and wheat, cattle and sheep, horses and chariots, and bodies and souls of men. ¹⁴The fruit that your soul longed for has gone from you, and all the things which are rich and splendid have ᵃgone from you, and you shall find them no more at all. ¹⁵The merchants of these things, who became rich by her, will stand at a distance for fear of her torment, weeping and wailing, ¹⁶and saying, 'Alas, alas, that great city that was clothed in fine linen, purple, and scarlet, and adorned with gold and precious stones and pearls! ¹⁷For in one hour such great riches ᵃcame to nothing.' Every shipmaster, all who travel by ship, sailors, and as many as trade on the sea, stood at a distance ¹⁸and cried out when they saw the smoke of her burning, saying, 'What *is* like this great city?'

¹⁹"They threw dust on their heads and cried out, weeping and wailing, and saying, 'Alas, alas, that great city, in which all who had ships on the sea became rich by her wealth! For in one hour she ᵃis made desolate.'

²⁰"Rejoice over her, O heaven, and *you* ᵃholy apostles and prophets, for God has avenged you on her!"

---

18:14 ᵃ NU, M *been lost to you*   18:17 ᵃ *have been laid waste*   18:19 ᵃ *have been laid waste*   18:20 ᵃ NU, M *saints and apostles*

**18:9–20** Describes the outcome of the sentence pronounced in vv. 5–8 in the style of an ancient lament (see Lamentations; Ezek. 27).

**18:9–10 *kings of the earth . . . weep.*** The political rulers of the world caused Babylon's destruction (17:16) but now mourn the loss of power, position, and prestige they enjoyed with her. ***lived luxuriously with her.*** See 17:2. ***one hour.*** Expresses the rapidity of the final destruction (compare 18:17, 19).

**18:11 *merchants of the earth.*** The economic side of Babylon was not emphasized in chap. 17.

**18:12–13** Similar list in Ezek. 27:12–22.

**18:16 *clothed.*** See 17:4–5. ***fine linen.*** The dress of the righteous (19:8, 14). Babylon uses a Christian face to deceive the world (16:14). See note on 17:4–5.

**18:18 *like this.*** See note on 13:4.

**18:19 *threw dust.*** Expression of great sorrow (see Ezek. 27:30).

**18:20** Babylon's fall described from the perspective of her victims.

### Finality of Babylon's Fall

²¹Then a mighty angel took up a stone like a great millstone and threw *it* into the sea, saying, "Thus with violence the great city Babylon shall be thrown down, and shall not be found anymore. ²²The sound of harpists, musicians, flutists, and trumpeters shall not be heard in you anymore. No craftsman of any craft shall be found in you anymore, and the sound of a millstone shall not be heard in you anymore. ²³The light of a lamp shall not shine in you anymore, and the voice of bridegroom and bride shall not be heard in you anymore. For your merchants were the great men of the earth, for by your sorcery all the nations were deceived. ²⁴And in her was found the blood of prophets and saints, and of all who were slain on the earth."

### Heaven Exults over Babylon

**19** After these things I ᵃheard a loud voice of a great multitude in heaven, saying, "Alleluia! Salvation and glory and honor and power *belong* to ᵇthe Lord our God! ²For true and righteous *are* His judgments, because He has judged the great harlot who corrupted the earth with her fornication; and He has avenged on her the blood of His servants *shed* by her." ³Again they said, "Alleluia! Her smoke rises up forever and ever!" ⁴And the twenty-four elders and the four living creatures fell down and worshiped God who sat on the throne, saying, "Amen! Alleluia!" ⁵Then a voice came from the throne, saying, "Praise our God, all you His servants and those who fear Him, both ᵃ small and great!"

⁶And I heard, as it were, the voice of a great multitude, as the sound of many waters and as the sound of mighty thunderings, saying, "Alleluia! For the ᵃ Lord God Omnipotent reigns! ⁷Let us be glad and rejoice and give Him glory, for the marriage of the Lamb has come, and His wife has made herself ready." ⁸And to her it was granted to be arrayed in fine linen, clean and bright, for the fine linen is the righteous acts of the saints.

---

19:1 ᵃ NU, M add *something like*   ᵇ NU, M omit *the Lord*   19:5 ᵃ NU, M omit *both*   19:6 ᵃ NU, M *our*

**18:21–24** The finality of Babylon's fall.

**18:21** Recalls Jer. 51:59–64.

**18:22–23** Babylon's fall is complete—no more music, workmanship, food production, or marriage. **bridegroom.** Contrast 19:7–9. **sorcery.** Delusion through illusion. See 9:21; 21:8; 22:15. **deceived.** See 13:13–14; 16:14; 19:20.

**18:24 blood.** See 6:10; 17:6; 19:2. The main ground for Babylon's punishment is the way she treated God's people.

**19:1–5** Elaborates the celebration over Babylon's fall in 18:20. The actions that destroyed Babylon in chap. 18 also delivered the people of God.

**19:1 great multitude.** See 7:9–17. **Alleluia.** Based on the Hebrew word for "praise the Lord." **Salvation . . . our God.** Recalls 7:10, 12.

**19:2 true . . . judgments.** Recalls the wording of 15:3–4 and 16:5–7. For other attributes of God the Father, see Ex. 34:6–7. **judged . . . avenged.** This text announces the final fulfillment of what was requested in Rev. 6:9–10. For more on judgment, see Dan. 7:9–14, 22, 26–27. **great harlot . . . fornication.** Recalls 17:1–6.

**19:3 smoke . . . ever.** Recalls 14:11. In chap. 14 individuals are in view; here it is Babylon as a corporate body that is judged.

**19:4 twenty-four elders . . . living creatures.** See notes on 4:4–8.

**19:5 small and great.** See note on 13:16–17.

**19:7 wife . . . ready.** Weddings are ready when the groom, the bride, and the place are prepared. The focus here is on the readiness of the bride; in John 14:1–3 the focus is on the readiness of the place. See also Hos. 2:19–20; Eph. 5:31–32.

**19:8 fine linen.** See 18:12, 16; 19:14. Defined as "the righteous acts of the saints." God's end-time people will be fully loyal and obedient to Him. See 12:17, 14:12, and note on 14:7. **clean and bright.** See 15:6. **saints.** See 21:9–10; Heb. 12:22–23. City and bride are two symbols for the people of God.

⁹Then he said to me, "Write: 'Blessed *are* those who are called to the marriage supper of the Lamb!' " And he said to me, "These are the true sayings of God." ¹⁰And I fell at his feet to worship him. But he said to me, "See *that you do* not *do that!* I am your fellow servant, and of your brethren who have the testimony of Jesus. Worship God! For the testimony of Jesus is the spirit of prophecy."

### Christ on a White Horse

¹¹Now I saw heaven opened, and behold, a white horse. And He who sat on him *was* called Faithful and True, and in righteousness He judges and makes war. ¹²His eyes *were* like a flame of fire, and on His head *were* many crowns. He ᵃhad a name written that no one knew except Himself. ¹³He *was* clothed with a robe dipped in blood, and His name is called The Word of God. ¹⁴And the armies in heaven, clothed in ᵃfine linen, white and clean, followed Him on white horses. ¹⁵Now out of His mouth goes a ᵃsharp sword, that with it He should strike the nations. And He Himself will rule them with a rod of iron. He Himself treads the winepress of the fierceness and wrath of Almighty God. ¹⁶And He has on *His* robe and on His thigh a name written:

KING OF KINGS
AND LORD OF LORDS.

### The Beast and His Armies Defeated

¹⁷Then I saw an angel standing in the sun; and he cried with a loud voice, saying to all the birds that fly in the midst of heaven, "Come and gather together for the ᵃsupper of the great God, ¹⁸that you may eat the flesh of kings, the flesh of captains, the flesh of mighty men, the flesh of horses and of those who sit on them, and the flesh of all *people,* ᵃfree and slave, both small and great."

---

19:12 ᵃ M adds *names written, and*   19:14 ᵃ NU, M *pure white linen*   19:15 ᵃ M *sharp two-edged*
19:17 ᵃ NU, M *great supper of God*   19:18 ᵃ NU, M *both free*

**19:9 Blessed.** See note on 1:3.

**19:10** Compare 22:8–9. *your brethren.* Called "prophets" in 22:9. ***testimony of Jesus.*** See notes on 1:2 and 12:17. The testimony of Jesus is the prophetic gift. On other spiritual gifts, see Rom. 12:4–8; 1 Cor. 12:7–10, 27–30; Eph. 4:11–16.

**19:11** This verse answers the question of 13:4. ***heaven opened.*** See 4:1. ***white horse.*** See note on 6:2.

**19:12** Another description of Jesus. ***flame of fire.*** See 1:14. ***many crowns.*** These are royal crowns, in contrast to 6:2. ***no one knew.*** There are aspects of Christ's character too deep for us to understand.

**19:13** ***dipped in blood.*** Either that of the enemy (14:14–20; Is. 63:1–3) or the atoning blood of Christ. **The Word of God.** See John 1:1–5, 14.

**19:14** ***fine linen.*** See note on v. 8.

**19:15** ***sharp sword . . . rod of iron.*** Images of Jesus in Revelation (1:16; 2:27; 12:5). The rod of iron is a scepter, which is a symbol of royal authority. ***strike the nations.*** See 14:17–20; 16:17–21. Babylon was dealt with in chaps. 17–18; the attention here is on the rest of the wicked. ***winepress.*** See 14:17–20.

**19:16** ***king . . . lords.*** See 17:14. This scene completes what was begun in 17:12–17.

**19:17–18** ***supper.*** See Ezek. 39:17–20. Contrast Rev. 19:9. ***free . . . great.*** Recalls 6:15. These verses emphasize the final destruction of earth's political and military powers.

¹⁹And I saw the beast, the kings of the earth, and their armies, gathered together to make war against Him who sat on the horse and against His army. ²⁰Then the beast was captured, and with him the false prophet who worked signs in his presence, by which he deceived those who received the mark of the beast and those who worshiped his image. These two were cast alive into the lake of fire burning with brimstone. ²¹And the rest were killed with the sword which proceeded from the mouth of Him who sat on the horse. And all the birds were filled with their flesh.

### Satan Bound 1,000 Years

**20** Then I saw an angel coming down from heaven, having the key to the bottomless pit and a great chain in his hand. ²He laid hold of the dragon, that serpent of old, who is *the* Devil and Satan, and bound him for a thousand years; ³and he cast him into the bottomless pit, and shut him up, and set a seal on him, so that he should deceive the nations no more till the thousand years were finished. But after these things he must be released for a little while.

### The Saints Reign with Christ 1,000 Years

⁴And I saw thrones, and they sat on them, and judgment was committed to them. Then *I saw* the souls of those who had been beheaded for their witness to Jesus and for the word of God, who had not worshiped the beast or his image, and had not received *his* mark on their foreheads or on their hands. And they lived and reigned with Christ for ᵃa thousand years. ⁵But the rest of the dead did not live again until the thousand years were finished. This *is* the first resurrection. ⁶Blessed and holy *is* he who has part in the first resurrection. Over such the second death has no power, but they shall be priests of God and of Christ, and shall reign with Him a thousand years.

---

**20:4** ᵃ M *the*

**19:19 beast . . . earth.** Reference to the war of 17:14. The beast and kings represent the secular, political powers of the world.

**19:20 beast . . . false prophet.** Component systems of Babylon (see 16:13, 19) are destroyed at the Second Advent. **who worked . . . image.** See 13:13–17. **lake of fire.** See 20:14–15.

**20:1–15** The Millennium, or one thousand years, is a unique contribution of this chapter. The Millennium is clearly after the Second Coming because it presupposes the false worship of the beast and its image and mark of the beast of chaps. 12–19. It connects with the rest of the biblical picture of the end as follows: at the Second Coming of Jesus, the wicked are destroyed (19:21; 2 Thess. 1:7–8) and the saints go to heaven (John 14:1–3). For a thousand years Satan is confined to this earth (Rev. 20:1–3) while the earth itself lies ruined and desolate (v. 5; Jer. 4:23–27) and the saints are judging in heaven (John 14:1–3; 1 Cor. 6:2–3). At the end of the thousand years, the New Jerusalem comes down from heaven (Rev. 21:2; 20:9), the wicked are resurrected (v. 5), Satan is released to deceive the nations and attack the city (vv. 7–9), and the wicked are judged and destroyed by fire (vv. 9–15). There are only two other passages in the Bible that seem to address what happens after the Second Coming of Jesus but before the new earth: Isa. 24:19–22 and 1 Cor. 15:22–24.

**20:1 key . . . pit.** See note on 9:1.

**20:2 the dragon . . . Satan.** See notes on 12:7–9.

**20:3 cast him . . . shut him up.** Reversal of 9:1–11. **must be released.** Satan's release serves God's purpose as a final demonstration of the character of sin and its consequences.

**20:4–5** This passage presents an important glimpse of some of what takes place in heaven after the Second Coming of Christ. **judgment.** See 1 Cor. 6:2–3. **beheaded.** Implies a physical death and resurrection. These resurrections are at the Second Coming; they are not spiritual resurrections in response to the preaching of the gospel. **their witness . . . God.** See Rev. 6:9. **worshiped . . . hands.** See 13:15–17. **lived.** Physical resurrection. For more on the resurrection, see Matt. 24:31; 1 Cor. 15:51–55; 1 Thess. 4:15–17. **reigned with Christ.** See Rev. 7:15–17. For more events connected to the Millennium, see John 14:3; 1 Cor. 6:2–3; Rev. 21:1–5. See also note on 20:1–15. **the rest of the dead.** The wicked.

**20:6 Blessed.** See note on 1:3. **first resurrection.** Of all of the righteous at the Second Coming. The wicked are not resurrected until the end of the thousand years (20:5). **second death.** See note on v. 14. **priests . . . reign.** See 1:5–6; 5:10.

## Satanic Rebellion Crushed
*(cf. Ezek. 38; 39)*

⁷Now when the thousand years have expired, Satan will be released from his prison ⁸and will go out to deceive the nations which are in the four corners of the earth, Gog and Magog, to gather them together to battle, whose number *is* as the sand of the sea. ⁹They went up on the breadth of the earth and surrounded the camp of the saints and the beloved city. And fire came down from God out of heaven and devoured them. ¹⁰The devil, who deceived them, was cast into the lake of fire and brimstone where ᵃ the beast and the false prophet *are*. And they will be tormented day and night forever and ever.

## The Great White Throne Judgment

¹¹Then I saw a great white throne and Him who sat on it, from whose face the earth and the heaven fled away. And there was found no place for them. ¹²And I saw the dead, small and great, standing before ᵃ God, and books were opened. And another book was opened, which is *the Book* of Life. And the dead were judged according to their works, by the things which were written in the books. ¹³The sea gave up the dead who were in it, and Death and Hades delivered up the dead who were in them. And they were judged, each one according to his works. ¹⁴Then Death and Hades were cast into the lake of fire. This is the second ᵃ death. ¹⁵And anyone not found written in the Book of Life was cast into the lake of fire.

---

20:10 ᵃ NU, M *where also*   20:12 ᵃ NU, M *the throne*   20:14 ᵃ NU, M *death, the lake of fire.*

**20:7 when . . . expired.** Although not mentioned here, we know from v. 5 that the wicked dead are raised at this time. **prison.** Vv. 1–3.

**20:8 Gog and Magog.** Symbolizes the wicked in rebellion against God. See Ezek. 38–39. **gather . . . to battle.** Recalls Armageddon (Rev. 16:14, 16). **the sand . . . sea.** All the wicked who ever lived. Contrast Gen. 22:17.

**20:9 beloved city.** Described in detail in chap. 21. This scene happens after the city comes down from heaven (21:2).

**20:10 devil.** The first intelligent being to be destroyed is the father of the rebellion (12:7–9). **lake of fire.** See vv. 14–15; 19:20; compare Gen. 19:24. **beast . . . prophet.** His existence is at an end as definitively as his systems of belief one thousand years earlier (see note on 19:20). **tormented . . . forever.** See notes on 14:9–11.

**20:11 earth . . . fled.** Poetic description of the earth's destruction by fire. See 2 Pet. 3:10–12.

**20:12 dead.** The wicked dead. The righteous are already saved and in the city. **books.** Books of evidence upon which the fate of the wicked is confirmed. **Book of Life.** This is when Phil. 2:10–11 will be fulfilled and the justice of God will be recognized by the whole cosmos, including the wicked and Satan himself. For more on the books used in judgment, see Rev. 3:5; Ex. 32:33; Mal. 3:16–18; Luke 10:20; Phil. 4:3.

**20:13 sea . . . Death and Hades.** The universality of this resurrection; includes all the wicked who ever lived. **Hades.** The grave (Job 17:13; Song 8:6). **according to his works.** 2 Cor. 5:10.

**20:14 Death . . . fire.** To some degree the lake of fire is figurative. The text is saying there will be no more death and no more grave. **second death.** The permanent penalty for sin, eternal separation from God. The saved are exempt from this (vv. 6, 15). Death signifies nonexistence rather than endless torture. For more on hell and the punishment of the wicked, see Matt. 3:12; 13:42; 25:41; Mark 9:43.

## All Things Made New

**21** Now I saw a new heaven and a new earth, for the first heaven and the first earth had passed away. Also there was no more sea. ²Then I, ᵃJohn, saw the holy city, New Jerusalem, coming down out of heaven from God, prepared as a bride adorned for her husband. ³And I heard a loud voice from heaven saying, "Behold, the tabernacle of God *is* with men, and He will dwell with them, and they shall be His people. God Himself will be with them *and be* their God. ⁴And God will wipe away every tear from their eyes; there shall be no more death, nor sorrow, nor crying. There shall be no more pain, for the former things have passed away."

⁵Then He who sat on the throne said, "Behold, I make all things new." And He said ᵃto me, "Write, for these words are true and faithful."

⁶And He said to me, "It ᵃ is done! I am the Alpha and the Omega, the Beginning and the End. I will give of the fountain of the water of life freely to him who thirsts. ⁷He who overcomes ᵃshall inherit all things, and I will be his God and he shall be My son. ⁸But the cowardly, ᵃunbelieving, abominable, murderers, sexually immoral, sorcerers, idolaters, and all liars shall have their part in the lake which burns with fire and brimstone, which is the second death."

## The New Jerusalem
*(cf. Ezek. 48:30–35)*

⁹Then one of the seven angels who had the seven bowls filled with the seven last plagues came ᵃto me and talked with me, saying, "Come, I will show you the ᵇbride, the Lamb's wife." ¹⁰And he carried me away in the Spirit to a great and high mountain, and showed me the ᵃgreat city, the ᵇholy Jerusalem, descending out of heaven from God, ¹¹having the glory of God. Her light *was* like a most precious stone, like a jasper stone, clear as crystal.

---

**21:2** ᵃ NU, M omit *John*   **21:5** ᵃ NU, M omit *to me*   **21:6** ᵃ M omits *It is done*   **21:7** ᵃ M *I shall give him these things*   **21:8** ᵃ M adds *and sinners,*   **21:9** ᵃ NU, M omit *to me*   ᵇ M *woman, the Lamb's bride*   **21:10** ᵃ NU, M omit *great*   ᵇ NU, M *holy city, Jerusalem*

**21:1–8** This section is the climax of chap. 20, but it also serves as the introduction to the New Jerusalem vision (21:9—22:5).

**21:1 new heaven.** A re-creation of what was created in Gen. 1:1. **new earth.** See 7:16–17; Is. 11:6–9; 35:4–10; 65:17, 21–25; 2 Pet. 3:13. **no more sea.** Such as the oceans we have today. Does not rule out smaller bodies of water in the New Earth.

**21:2 the holy city.** The description combines elements of OT Jerusalem, its temple (1 Kin. 6–8), and the garden of Eden (Gen. 1–3). **coming down . . . heaven.** See John 14:1–3. The place Jesus is preparing for His people only comes to earth after the one thousand years, known as the Millennium. See Rev. 20:4–6. **bride.** See 19:7–8. The bride is a city full of saved people.

**21:3 tabernacle.** Recalls the Mosaic tabernacle (Ex. 25–40). Fulfills the covenant language of Ezek. 37:26–28.

**21:4 wipe away every tear.** See 7:17. Recovering from the past can take time.

**21:6 Alpha . . . End.** See note on 1:8. **water of life freely.** Anticipates 22:1–5. See note on 22:17.

**21:7 He who overcomes.** Recalls the promises of chaps. 2–3. See note on 2:7.

**21:8** A list of those excluded from the city. See also v. 27; 22:15. The Bible does not teach universal salvation. **cowardly.** Not the naturally timid; this refers to those who choose personal safety over faithfulness to God in the end time. **abominable.** Associated with idolatry. **lake . . . death.** See note on 20:14.

**21:9—22:5** The New Jerusalem is described as if approaching from a distance, with details coming more and more into focus.

**21:9 one of . . . plagues.** See 15:1–8; 17:1. This sets up a series of contrasts between Babylon, the harlot, and Jerusalem, the bride of the Lamb. **bride.** See 19:7–8 and note on 21:2.

**21:10 in the Spirit.** See note on 1:10. **descending out of heaven.** Returns to 21:2. The appearance of this New Jerusalem signals the completion of the fall of Babylon/Cyrus theme that began in chap. 16. See note on 16:12.

**21:11 jasper . . . crystal.** See note on v. 18; see also 4:3–6.

¹²Also she had a great and high wall with twelve gates, and twelve angels at the gates, and names written on them, which are *the names* of the twelve tribes of the children of Israel: ¹³three gates on the east, three gates on the north, three gates on the south, and three gates on the west.

¹⁴Now the wall of the city had twelve foundations, and on them were the ᵃnames of the twelve apostles of the Lamb. ¹⁵And he who talked with me had a gold reed to measure the city, its gates, and its wall. ¹⁶The city is laid out as a square; its length is as great as its breadth. And he measured the city with the reed: twelve thousand ᵃfurlongs. Its length, breadth, and height are equal. ¹⁷Then he measured its wall: one hundred *and* forty-four cubits, *according* to the measure of a man, that is, of an angel. ¹⁸The construction of its wall was *of* jasper; and the city *was* pure gold, like clear glass. ¹⁹The foundations of the wall of the city *were* adorned with all kinds of precious stones: the first foundation *was* jasper, the second sapphire, the third chalcedony, the fourth emerald, ²⁰the fifth sardonyx, the sixth sardius, the seventh chrysolite, the eighth beryl, the ninth topaz, the tenth chrysoprase, the eleventh jacinth, and the twelfth amethyst. ²¹The twelve gates *were* twelve pearls: each individual gate was of one pearl. And the street of the city *was* pure gold, like transparent glass.

### The Glory of the New Jerusalem

²²But I saw no temple in it, for the Lord God Almighty and the Lamb are its temple. ²³The city had no need of the sun or of the moon to shine ᵃin it, for the ᵇglory of God illuminated it. The Lamb *is* its light. ²⁴And the nations ᵃof those who are saved shall walk in its light, and the kings of the earth bring their glory and honor ᵇinto it. ²⁵Its gates shall not be shut at all by day (there shall be no night there). ²⁶And they shall bring the glory and the honor of the nations into ᵃit. ²⁷But there shall by no means enter

---

21:14 ᵃ NU, M *twelve names*   21:16 ᵃ Lit. *stadia*, about 1,380 miles in all   21:23 ᵃ NU, M omit *in it*   ᵇ M *very glory*   21:24 ᵃ NU, M omit *of those who are saved*   ᵇ M *of the nations to Him*   21:26 ᵃ M adds *that they may enter in.*

**21:12–14 gates . . . twelve tribes.** See Ezek. 48:30–35. Along with the twelve foundations, both OT and NT people of God are represented. **apostles.** See Eph. 2:20. The New Jerusalem has twelve foundations, each named to serve as a reminder of what the city's purpose is.

**21:15 rod.** See Ezek. 48:30–35 and note on 11:1. In those passages the temple of God is measured. With the glory of God at its center, the New Jerusalem itself functions as the temple (see 21:22).

**21:16 twelve thousand furlongs.** It is not clear if that measurement is of each side of the city or of all four sides combined. The same descriptive measurement could apply to a cube or a pyramid. The Most Holy Place of Solomon's Temple (1 Kin. 6:20) had the measurements of a cube. On the other hand, a pyramid could be representative of a mountain, such as Mount Zion (Rev. 14:1), a dwelling place for God.

**21:17 one hundred and forty-four.** See 7:4–8; 14:1. **cubits.** A cubit was the length from a man's elbow to the fingertips.

**21:18 jasper.** A variety of quartz, usually red.

**21:19–20** The gems here correspond generally to the gems in the breastplate of the OT high priest. The privileges of direct access to God that were reserved for the high priest are now freely available to all God's people.

**21:21 pearls.** Extremely valuable in the ancient world. **street . . . gold.** The floor of Solomon's temple was overlaid with gold (1 Kin. 6:30).

**21:22 no temple.** Contrast 7:15. The earlier text reflects the situation in heaven during the Millennium. Here the symbol has given way to the reality of God's direct presence (21:23; 22:1–4) after the Millennium.

**21:23** Recalls 21:11; Is. 60:19–20.

**21:24–26** Isaiah saw the same thing and recorded it in Is. 60:3–14. **gates shall not be shut.** Indicates universal access and safety. Everything that could threaten the city and its inhabitants has been defeated.

**21:27** See note on 21:8. **Book of Life.** See note on 3:5.

it anything <sup>a</sup>that defiles, or causes an abomination or a lie, but only those who are written in the Lamb's Book of Life.

## The River of Life

**22** And he showed me a <sup>a</sup>pure river of water of life, clear as crystal, proceeding from the throne of God and of the Lamb. ²In the middle of its street, and on either side of the river, *was* the tree of life, which bore twelve fruits, each *tree* yielding its fruit every month. The leaves of the tree *were* for the healing of the nations. ³And there shall be no more curse, but the throne of God and of the Lamb shall be in it, and His servants shall serve Him. ⁴They shall see His face, and His name *shall be* on their foreheads. ⁵There shall be no night there: They need no lamp nor light of the sun, for the Lord God gives them light. And they shall reign forever and ever.

## The Time Is Near

⁶Then he said to me, "These words *are* faithful and true." And the Lord God of the <sup>a</sup>holy prophets sent His angel to show His servants the things which must shortly take place.

⁷"Behold, I am coming quickly! Blessed *is* he who keeps the words of the prophecy of this book."

⁸Now I, John, <sup>a</sup>saw and heard these things. And when I heard and saw, I fell down to worship before the feet of the angel who showed me these things.

⁹Then he said to me, "See *that you do* not *do that.* <sup>a</sup>For I am your fellow servant, and of your brethren the prophets, and of those who keep the words of this book. Worship God." ¹⁰And he said to me, "Do not seal the words of the prophecy of this book, for the time is at hand. ¹¹He who is unjust, let him be unjust still; he who is filthy, let him be filthy still; he who is righteous, let him <sup>a</sup>be righteous still; he who is holy, let him be holy still."

---

21:27 <sup>a</sup> NU, M *profane, nor one who causes*   22:1 <sup>a</sup> NU, M omit *pure*   22:6 <sup>a</sup> NU, M *spirits of the prophets*
22:8 <sup>a</sup> NU, M *am the one who heard and saw*   22:9 <sup>a</sup> NU, M omit *For*   22:11 <sup>a</sup> NU, M *do right*

**22:1** *river . . . life.* Recalls Gen. 2:8–14; Ezek. 47:1–12; Zech. 14:8; John 7:37–39. *the throne . . . of the Lamb.* The first time this phrase is used in Revelation (it is used again in 22:3). The Lamb's role is clearly implied by 3:21.

**22:2** *tree of life.* See 2:7; Gen. 2:9; 3:22. *fruit every month.* Recalls Is. 66:22–23 and Ezek. 47:12. *healing of the nations.* Probably the perfect reconciliation of cultures and ethnic groups because of the final elimination of all traces of selfishness and sin.

**22:3** *no more curse.* Gen. 3:14–19. Salvation has finally undone all traces of Adam's sin. *servants . . . Him.* See Rev. 7:15.

**22:4** *They shall see His face.* The best thing about eternal life is intimate relationship with the greatest of all personalities. *name . . . foreheads.* See note on 14:1. Contrast 13:16–17.

**22:6** *faithful and true.* Similar words were used to describe Jesus in 3:14 and 19:11. Applied to the words of Revelation also in 21:6. The book of Revelation is as reliable as Jesus is. *must shortly take place.* See note on 1:1.

**22:7** *I am coming quickly!* See vv. 12, 20; 3:11; and note on 1:1. *Blessed.* See note on 1:3.

**22:8–9** A comparison with 19:10 shows that prophets have the testimony of Jesus (see 12:17). *saw.* John also saw the testimony of Jesus (1:2).

**22:10** *Do not seal the words.* Contrast Dan. 8:26; 12:4, 9. Most of the words of Revelation had immediate relevance to first-century readers and its prophecies were not to be sealed. *the time is at hand.* See note on Rev. 1:1.

**22:11** A striking description of the close of human probation at the end of history.

## Jesus Testifies to the Churches

¹²"And behold, I am coming quickly, and My reward *is* with Me, to give to every one according to his work. ¹³I am the Alpha and the Omega, *the* ᵃBeginning and *the* End, the First and the Last."

¹⁴Blessed *are* those who ᵃdo His commandments, that they may have the right to the tree of life, and may enter through the gates into the city. ¹⁵ᵃBut outside *are* dogs and sorcerers and sexually immoral and murderers and idolaters, and whoever loves and practices a lie.

¹⁶"I, Jesus, have sent My angel to testify to you these things in the churches. I am the Root and the Offspring of David, the Bright and Morning Star."

¹⁷And the Spirit and the bride say, "Come!" And let him who hears say, "Come!" And let him who thirsts come. Whoever desires, let him take the water of life freely.

## A Warning

¹⁸ᵃFor I testify to everyone who hears the words of the prophecy of this book: If anyone adds to these things, ᵇGod will add to him the plagues that are written in this book; ¹⁹and if anyone takes away from the words of the book of this prophecy, Godᵃ shall take away his part from the ᵇBook of Life, from the holy city, and *from* the things which are written in this book.

## I Am Coming Quickly

²⁰He who testifies to these things says, "Surely I am coming quickly."

Amen. Even so, come, Lord Jesus!

²¹The grace of our Lord Jesus Christ *be* ᵃwith you all. Amen.

---

**22:13** ᵃ NU, M *First and the Last, the Beginning and the End.*   **22:14** ᵃ NU *wash their robes,*   **22:15** ᵃ NU, M omit *But*   **22:18** ᵃ NU, M omit *For*   ᵇ M *may God add*   **22:19** ᵃ M *may God take away*   ᵇ NU, M *tree of life*   **22:21** ᵃ NU *with all;* M *with all the saints*

**22:12 I am coming quickly.** See note on v. 7. **reward . . . work.** See 20:12–13; 2 Cor. 5:10. We are justified by faith, but the evidence of faith is in the works that follow justification. See James 2:18–22.

**22:13** Here Jesus carries the same titles as the Father in 1:8, affirming His full equality with God.

**22:14 Blessed.** See note on 1:3.

**22:15** See note on 21:8. **dogs.** Often used negatively in the ancient world. See Deut. 23:17–18; Matt. 15:26–27; Phil. 3:2.

**22:16 in the churches.** Literally "for" or "to" the churches. The entire book is relevant to the experience of the churches. **the Root . . . of David.** See Is. 11:1, 10. Jesus is both the ancestor and the descendant of David, the messianic king. **the Bright and Morning Star.** See Num. 24:17. Once again, in Rev. 22:16–21, the three members of the Godhead or Trinity are mentioned in relation to one another (God the Father, vv. 18–19; Jesus, vv. 16, 20–21; Holy Spirit, v. 17). See 1:4–5; 4:2, 5; 5:5–6.

**22:17 bride.** See 19:7–8; 21:2, 9–10. **water of life freely.** While those who love God long to obey Him, salvation is truly free.

**22:18–19** While written with Revelation in mind, this warning is appropriate to all of Scripture. **prophecy.** For more on the prophetic origin of the Bible, see 2 Tim. 3:15–17; Heb. 1:1; 2 Pet. 1:20–21.

**22:20–21 I am coming quickly.** See note on v. 7. **grace.** While Revelation discloses judgments and plagues, it focuses on the salvation offered by God and emphasizes grace at the beginning (1:4) and end.

# Broaden your scope...

The study notes in this volume are from the *Andrews Study Bible* (NKJV edition). Why not get the rest of the study notes by purchasing the entire study Bible? The *Andrews Study Bible* is available in both the New King James Version and the New International Version.

# Deepen your knowledge...

The *Andrews Bible Commentary* is a concise commentary to complement the *Andrews Study Bible*. Get outstanding insights presented by some sixty biblical experts from around the world in this landmark new resource for the Church.

# Order these two great resources today:

Adventist Book Center:
(800) 765–6955
Andrews University Press:
(800) 467–6369 or universitypress.andrews.edu